Are You Culturally Competent?

Clinicians discuss the relevance of cultural competency in their practices.

by

Elisa P. Bell, M.D.

Are You Culturally Competent?

Elisa P. Bell, M.D.

ISBN: 978-1-09830-415-7

Table of Contents

Dedication

This work is in memory of my grandmother—Annie Binford, my mother—Acelene Marie Bell, and my godmother—Mrs. Lynda Beverly. These women are my guardian angels. My life springs from their words of wisdom, nurturance, and "sister" talk, a tradition of the southern way. They gave and give me confidence in self and work, when I had no idea of the power I possessed.

Acknowledgements

I would like to thank my dear friends: Dr. Morris Blount, Dr. Joyce Miller, Dr. Diane Washington, Dr. Beatrice Brewer, Dr. Stan Blom, and Dr. Lynne Mock for their contributions in writing cultural competency cases as well as their support in completing this challenging task. I would also like to thank Francoie Jolie, Arnell Brady, and Dr. Victor Tan for their excellence in their fields, caring for their patients, and their contributions to my book. These professionals have taken time out of their very busy schedules to share their experiences and expertise in the field of cultural competency.

I had the pleasure of meeting the National Director of Cultural Competency, Tawara D. Goode, and her Vice President, Suzanne Bronheim Ph.D., at the Center for Human Development in Washington, DC. They embraced me, allowing me to record and share my interviews with them. They gave me resources to read and instructions on cultural competency. Our meetings encouraged progress and added details for this book to enhance its evolution.

I discovered an intriguing personality in Dr. Brian Griffin. It was a blessing to encounter him at Cleveland Clinic. His life experiences and practice provide a model for this book. Our interview was informative, honest, meaningful, and brought me tears of joy. He understands culture and the compelling need for all of us to become more culturally competent.

God puts us in places at the right time to receive our blessings. While in Ethiopia, I met and had several conversations with Reverend Otis Moss, Jr. His kindness, wisdom, and humble spirit supported his humanitarian tasks and goals--being in his presence was an honor. In addition, I need to thank my dear friend Ms. Shirley Clay whose prayers and support were beacons when doubt was heavy.

I am often told that I have a spirit similar to my adopted god-mother, Mrs. Jerrie Blakley—a wonderful compliment. She is a mother, friend and a blessing to everyone she encounters. I know her, I respect her, and I cherish her. Her acceptance and guidance have ordered my steps throughout the years. I love her dearly.

A very blessed thanks to my inspiring mentor, Dr. Carl C. Bell. He has given me valued instruction, unfailingly supported my career and granted me freedom to learn and grow since we first met in 1991. My thanks to Dr. Bell will always be continuous, and I am honored to know him.

My friends Francene Pelmon and Paul Butler (Eric) are special to me. They hold a candle for me and are present whenever I waiver or have a need. I love them both and offer them heartfelt thanks for their time and efforts. I have to thank God for the brother in Baltimore who has been called to preach God's word, Kevin Leonard; his help, support, and confidence in this project were essential. This work would not have been completed without him.

Finally, may I thank Superwoman, yes, Superwoman. She has patience, incredible ideas, and shows up and shows out when least expected. She is my editor and newfound friend, Michelle Thompson, JD. Thank you for being yourself and a vital part of this project. I could not have done it without you.

The next section was written by my dear friend and lifetime mentor, Dr. Carl Bell (no relation) who died before this book was published. I deeply regret that he could not be here to see this work come to pass. I miss him every day.

Foreword by Dr. Carl Bell

I first met Dr. Elisa Bell when she was completing her pediatrics residency at Loyola University. As a pediatric resident, she learned that many children who are presented to pediatricians for assistance need psychiatric care, something I have found to be quite common in this cohort of physicians. I suggested to her that she might think of doing a psychiatry residency followed by a child psychiatry residency at the Illinois State Psychiatric Institute, which was my alma mater and, at the time, the best adult residency training program in Chicago. She followed up by going to the University of Michigan Child Psychiatry Fellowship. While at U of M, she applied for a National Institute of Mental Health grant to study the problem of black-on-black crime in Chicago and Detroit, which I was very grateful for as I was also trying to address the issue and could have used all the help I could get. When she finished, I hired her as a child psychiatrist at the Community Mental Health Council, Inc. (a 22-million-dollar comprehensive community mental health center) to help with the desperately needed services for the African-American residents on Chicago's southeast and southwest sides. She worked there from 2000 to 2007.

Dr. Elisa Bell has always tried to help less fortunate people, and I have tried to support her in her efforts, as I think they are admirable. In this, her latest effort, she has gathered a number of diverse authors to provide an introductory perspective on cultural competence. Cultural competence is a very important aspect of medical and psychiatric care, as without it, health and mental health professionals would not be able to establish the best rapport possible with their patients. Accordingly, the book provides unique perspectives on the issue of how culture influences behavior.

Behavior is very complex because it is multi–determined. It has long been known that cultural, sociological, psychological, and bio-logical forces in a person's life determine behavior. Thanks to modern statistics (regression analysis), science has moved from comparing two of these variables to being able to take into account the influence of multiple variables at the same time. Accordingly, we have new models of human behavior such at the Theory of Triadic Influence that takes all of these variables into account when developing public health interventions for health behavior change.

For a physician/psychiatrist whose major reference point is biol-ogy, culture is one of the variables that is a bit more difficult to wrap one's head around. This book seeks to introduce the reader to the con-cept of culture and how important consideration of this variable is to develop rapport and understanding of what is driving a patient toward certain ways of thinking and behavior. Dr. Elisa Bell and her collection of authors have demonstrated a valuable lesson in the book—a person can be pro-one's culture and not anti-another culture.

Having done some population-based, health behavior change work in different cultures (most notably prevention of risky behaviors: violence, drug use, sexual behaviors), I have learned a few things about culture that may be instructive to the reader of this foreword.

I have never liked the term "minority" as it seems to define some-one who is automatically lesser than someone in the "majority," so I try to take a worldview, not a United States view. With a worldview, people of color are not in the "minority." I make a similar distinction when talking about slavery when I refer to the European-Americans who owned slaves as "owners" and not "masters."

I have learned that some cultures have destructive elements in them that may no longer support adaptation to life, and I have heard talk about "slave cultures" or "colonized cultures." Further, there are cultural characteristics of people that are destructive toward other cultures. For example, the European and European-American cultures are sometimes characterized as monocultural, ethnocentric cultures, which is the notion that the only culture that has ever produced anything of value is European-based.

In addition to the potential destructive elements of culture, there is the other side of the coin, culture can also be protective. Therefore, it is not the presence of a destructive culture causing harm to a group of people, but it's the absence of a destructive culture that protects people. This is a lesson I learned when doing HIV prevention research in Durban, South Africa where the Zulu people had HIV rates of 40%, the White South Africans had HIV rates of 6%, and the East Indian South Africans had HIV rates of 1%. Clearly, the East Indian South African culture was protecting itself by being specific on what to eat or not eat, who to pray to, how to get married, what clothes to wear, and other cultural influences.

Moving from a bigger picture to a smaller picture, cultural influences in a therapeutic clinical relationship are equally important. Chester M. Pierce, M.D., a former professor of Psychiatry, Public Health, and Education at Harvard, coined the terms microinsult and microaggression to capture the breaches in rapport between two people due to an encroachment on an individual's time, energy, mobility, and space. For example, imagine an African American C.E.O. of a $22 million comprehensive community mental health center going to an African American dermatologist and having a white, female receptionist asking him if he was going to pay with his medical card. Clearly, one major aspect of the process of refining one's "cultural competence" is not to make stereotypic assumptions about people perceived as different. Of course, the assumptions about people can be minor or extremely destructive.

While an undergraduate, I saw an advisor for course scheduling. The white academic advisor told me that the two-year plan I was working to graduate was ill-advised; he suggested I lower my sights to something more obtainable like auto mechanics. He did not know that my grandfather had gotten his first PhD from Yale in 1924, or that my father also had two PhDs. Therefore, the issue of cultural competence is not just important in mental health, but it is important in all aspects of life, especially since the world has gotten smaller due to the increased communication and exposure from the Internet.

A white male, Jewish, psychoanalytic colleague of mine told me of his analysis of a white, male, Catholic priest who was in treatment because of having obsessive sexual thoughts about another man's wife. After listening carefully for several years, the analyst finally told the priest, "Freud taught us that the thought is not the act." The priest told my colleague, "But I am Catholic. For me, the thought is the act!" This is an instance where a problem of cultural competence exists between two white, American males.

Mental health professionals are also surrounded by professional cultures that shape their perspectives on cause and effect. It has been argued that racism may be at the root of the high prevalence of preterm newborns in African American communities. Such hypotheses have existed in public health for some time; however, because birth outcomes are complex and multi-determined, it is important to consider alternative explanations that may be more amenable to intervention, i.e., acquired biology. Accordingly, an unconventional hypothesis is that racism shapes the social context of some African-Americans, putting them in situations where social determinates of health causes acquired biological disorders. For example, biological research has shown that many African American women do not know they are pregnant, and they may engage in social drinking causing fetal alcohol exposure, which is a major cause of prematurity and intellectual disability.

Lastly, to borrow a telling aphorism from Hayward Suggs, MBA, one of the former Senior Vice Presidents at the now defunct Community Mental Health Council on Chicago's South Side, "We are in the hard conversation business." Truer words were never spoken. Therapists and healers are in the hard conversation business, and we need to figure out the skills to have these conversations without destroying or damaging the therapeutic relationship. What is needed is a skill that is more than a notion, and takes into account the variable of culture.

Carl C. Bell, MD

Introduction

A big part of understanding a person's culture is to obtain their first-hand accounts regarding their community. With this in mind, I will share my cultural history.

In the 1950s and 1960s, Chicago's Lawndale community expanded across a twenty-nine-mile radius; to the east, the community was bordered by Western Avenue, and to the west, bordered by Pulaski Road. In the midst of those boundaries, I lived at 1445 South Millard.

For me, growing up in Lawndale during the 1960s was like living with relatives--our neighbors were extended family. The sixteen-block area where my grandparents allowed me to roam was a close-knit community--a village. And like the African proverb "It takes a village to rear a child," Chicago's Lawndale community fit that description.

My world as a child reached from my home to school, to the community park, to Grandma's grocery store, to my great-uncle's grocery store, to the local YMCA, to the church, and back home. These were the physical limits of my childhood roaming. This environment formulated my psyche; gave me my strong identity, my language, my beliefs, my celebrations, and my acceptance of self. The people in the Lawndale community shaped me, helping me with my mental, physical, emotional, psychological, social, spiritual, and cultural development.

Czechs first inhabited Lawndale in the 1800s, and between 1920 and 1955, twenty-five percent of Chicago's Jewish citizens occupied the community. In the 1950s, many African Americans migrated from southern states to Chicago, and some found homes in Lawndale. It was an industrial community with businesses like International Harvester, Sears Roebuck, Western Electric, Sunbeam, and Zenith. Residential housing included numerous grey-stone and two-flat brick buildings. With its jobs and housing, Lawndale was attractive to many.

In 1945, my family left their farm in Yazoo City, Mississippi and headed north to Chicago for a better life. My grandparents sought a fairer life for their children, and they wanted better work, and better housing. They were very industrious people; having only a sixth-grade education, they pushed forward by leaving the south. My grandparents joined the budding Lawndale community with hopes for a bright future.

My grandmother quickly became a pillar of the community; she was known to be fair and direct. My grandparents were deliberate and focused in their actions eventually owning two grey-stones, and a grocery store, "Mrs. Annie's." My grandmother would keep a ledger for monies our neighbors owed her when they purchased food and goods on credit. Every Monday, Wednesday, and Friday after school, I had to work at my grandmother's store. My responsibilities were to sweep, mop, and clean the back of the store for a whopping fifty cents a week. Up the street from my grandmother's grocery store were several churches, a barbershop, a liquor store, and numerous retail businesses on Roosevelt Road.

My grandmother's "prestige" largely related to our family's lineage--other Mississippi migrants knew of our family. We had the surnames Binford, Redmond, and Dixons—folks who were proud, hardworking people from Lexington County, Mississippi. There was respect and pride in being associated with my kinfolk. I was expected to behave well and respect myself and all elders. We were known as Christian folk who helped our neighbors. We were taught the "southern way" as children.

This meant having respectful manners, and acting as children under the direction of our elders. We greeted everyone, including strangers, politely and did not speak to elders unless addressed, and we dared not look elders in their eyes as this was also thought to be disrespectful.

Our church belief system was first in our lives (a collective consciousness and unconsciousness). We prayed together. We attended church regularly two to three times a week. Most of our community were "church-going folk," as we called them.

When a neighbor's child got into trouble by acting out, everyone knew it. An elder in the community would shower the child with parental advice and inform them that their parents would also be told about their behavior. If the behavior demanded immediate intervention, our neighbors or relatives would implement remediation or punishment. Our community thrived because of helpful "kinfolk," caring neighbors and close relatives.

As a child, my family lived in a three-flat brick apartment building on the third floor. Our elderly landlord, Mr. S., and his wife lived on the first floor.

The third floor had three bedrooms, a living room, a dining room, a kitchen, a back porch, and a large front deck. The front deck was where I spent much of my time daydreaming.

Our deck overlooked the community park and the roof of my school. People often frequented the park for picnics and walks, and I saw couples holding hands and kissing. I nicknamed the park "Lovers Lane." For me, the view from the deck was the best view in the world. I could see everything. Lawndale was my world, and I always felt a deep kinship for it; the community was ninety-nine percent black—populated by southerners, spiritual people, and proud people, creating a community, a village.

The Civil Rights Movement found kindred supporters in Lawndale including my grandparents. Caring community members met in churches, stores, and homes to encourage each other to seek fair housing, fair political representation, better jobs, and better schools. The community participated in activities to improve living conditions across the city.

In the late 1960s, work was limited for blacks in Chicago and almost nonexistent in Lawndale. As a result, Martin Luther King, Jr. selected Lawndale as a base for the northern Civil Rights Movement. Jesse Jackson Sr.'s Operation Breadbasket and Rainbow Push supported our village, as did the Black Panther Party fighting to create community. James Brown told us to "Say It Loud, I am Black and I am Proud," and Nina Simone instructed us "To Be Young, Gifted, and Black."

The day after Dr. Martin Luther King Jr.'s assassination remains a searing memory for me. I stood on my front deck and saw National Guard trucks rolling down my street. One truck tore through my schoolyard and a crowd of people. People scattered amid shouting and fighting with the soldiers. My beloved neighborhood was rioting.

My grandmother came over and went to my mother's room and closed the door behind her. I could hear her praying and crying, and she stayed in that room for two days. I heard her sobs and prayers the entire time. I realize now that my grandmother was coping by using the only tools she had, prayers and tears. Tears to relieve and prayers for hope. She isolated and then she prayed—the basis for my reality in the 1960s.

As a practicing physician for almost thirty years, I've treated many patients from myriad cultures, with distinct beliefs, traditions, rituals, languages, practices, faiths, and communities. I've learned to appreciate our differences. Better informed interactions with patients, including sharing, learning, asking questions, enhance trust and faith in the doctor-patient relationship.

On six continents I've been privileged to study specific cultures. I am fascinated by diversity and what makes up a community of people. In medicine our goal is to understand a patient's illness. I know now to look at my patient's cultural beliefs to learn how they see their illness as individuals, within their families and as part of a community culture. The more I learned about a patient's culture, family, and community, the more informed I became. This understanding of a patient's culture opened space for me to ask specific questions, and gave me much more information to make an accurate diagnosis, and therefore better treatment.

This book serves as an introduction to understanding culture, and how culture influences medical practice and why it is important for health practitioners to become more culturally competent. I reference and interview experts in the field and include anecdotes from skilled clinicians who discuss their cases in regard to their experiences and where they fall on the cultural competence spectrum. America is becoming more diverse. To communicate effectively and render a diagnosis to provide correct treatment, health practitioners must improve their cultural competency. Cultural competency is extremely important to anyone who serves in the medical profession, because it opens communication between practitioner and patient to get to the root of an illness or ailment and establish a correct diagnosis.

I intend to teach healthcare practitioners the importance of acknowledging and understanding the impact of culture in medical treatment. My hope is that practitioners understand that cultural competency is an absolute necessity. This work offers practitioners the basic steps to become more culturally competent.

Cultural competency is important to me as an African American woman, and as a physician. I have encountered medical professionals who had no clue how to engage and/or ask pertinent questions to recognize my humanity-- therefore, they made assumptions about me and my care.

I became ill during my second year of college and visited a free-standing clinic. I was diagnosed with pneumonia. The doctor told me to stop partying, to stop boozing, and to stop smoking. I attempted to tell the doctor that I was a premed student who never smoked or drank. I had been working long hours after classes, volunteering my time at a children's daycare and at a blood bank, and I had recently donated blood for a young boy's surgery. I tried to tell the doctor these details, but his eyes glazed over from his own erroneous assumptions: I was at a free clinic, an African American, (and he surmised) I had no regard for a healthy lifestyle, I was reckless and responsible for the infection. It was not hard to feel disrespected and unheard—he generalized me and demeaned my heritage with his assumptions.

I get very angry when I hear stories about medical professionals who do not engage with their patients. TR is a clinical psychologist and a dear friend and peer. Her twenty-nine-year-old son, JB, was shot in the head eight years ago. He has had a difficult recovery, and he still has major deficits. With the bullet lodged in his head, he was referred to an optho-neurologist due to the poor vision in his left eye. TR and her son had to wait months to see the specialist. The day of the appointment JB was examined for two hours by three medical students, one resident physician, and one fellow. The attending physician, Dr. P, did not examine him.

The group met to discuss JB's case for an additional two hours. When Dr. P finally spoke to JB, he told him, "My recommendation is that you do not get shot anymore." This statement speaks to Dr. P's assumption about JB's lifestyle. The doctor's—the healer's—words suggest that getting shot is a regular occurrence in any young African American man's life.

When I think about this interaction between my friend, her son, and the physician, I realize how badly our medical society needs to learn about cultural competency. We must intervene at medical schools, hospitals, urgent care facilities, nursing homes, and any other place where patients receive treatment. It is an absolute necessity.

Chapter One

Defining Cultural Competency

Along one's journey to becoming more culturally competent, a health-care provider will encounter terminology that may appear similar. For example, one may hear terms like diversity, multiculturalism, culture, race, and ethnicity. It is essential that learners are equipped with an understanding of the historical context in which these terms were created and how they have evolved. The following list of terms is not exhaustive, but it offers some basic awareness of the words and phrases that commonly appear in diversity training and conversations that center around cultural awareness.

Diversity:

The term diversity first appeared in America in the early forties. Diversity is defined as having people from different races, ethnic groups, and cultures in organizations and or programs.[1] In 1948, the first equal employment legislation was introduced to Congress. The Executive Order 9981 was signed by President Truman to desegregate

---

1   For a more detailed look at the definition of diversity visit the CUNY website: http://www.qcc.cuny. edu/diversity/definition.html

the armed forces. Even though this order required opportunity and equality of treatment for those enlisted in the armed forces, segregation continued.

In the 1960s, some twenty years later, the Civil Rights Movement occurred. Community cultural changes and social justice organizations brought about legislation such as the Civil Rights Act of 1964. "The Civil Rights Act of 1964 is a landmark Civil Rights and United States Labor Law, and it prohibits discrimination based on race, color, sex, or national origin."[2] During this time, there were increasing discrimination lawsuits, and diversity training was mandated for many businesses. Diversity training developed out of the need to comply with this new legislation. Phil Clements and John Jones define diversity as an "avoidance of monoculture."[3] A broader definition from the University of Maryland states that diversity is the "otherness, or human qualities that are different from our own and outside groups to which we belong, yet, are present in other individuals and groups."[4]

Multiculturalism:

Multiculturalism is one of the earliest terms used to describe multiple cultures living in a designated region. In 1957, Sweden was the first to put the term in print.[5] In the nineteenth century, there was a large immigration from southern and northern Europe to America. The term multiculturalism developed out of a necessity of such great change and differences among groups of migratory people.[6]

---

2   "Civil Rights Movement," *Wikipedia*, (May 2019): https://en.wikipedia.org/wiki/Civil_rights_movement
3   Phil Clements and John Jones, *The Diversity Training Handbook – A Practical Guide to Understanding and Changing Attitudes* (London: Kogan Page, 2012).
4   Ibid
5   "How Sweden Became Multicultural," *The Post Journal*, (May 2016): http://www.post-journal.com/life/2018/03/how-sweden-became-multicultural/
6   Phil Clements and John Jones, *The Diversity Training Handbook – A Practical Guide to Understanding and Changing Attitudes* (London: Kogan Page, 2012).

Elisa P. Bell, M.D.

My definition of multiculturalism refers to cultures existing and accepting each other within a given society. Whether that society is European, American, or Asian. For a brief explanation of multiculturalism, a culture existing within a society of different cultures, I will use the "southern way"—the cultural way in which I was raised.

As a child, we were taught not to look an adult in the eye, to address adults with sir and ma'am. Girls were taught to sit with their knees together and their ankles crossed. And in general, children were seen and not heard. These behavioral actions were different from the larger American culture. For the most part, American children are loud and rambunctious, and they are often daring and challenging to adults. This is contrary to children raised the southern way; however, the southern way of raising a child continues to exist within the larger American society. It is not attacked or ridiculed; it exists within the whole adding to the multiculturalism of a society.

Accepting is key to having a functional multicultural society. Historically, America has only been accepting out of necessity. When workers were needed, foreign enclaves were allowed to take root into communities, Chinatowns for example, but the communities were often ostracized and not viewed as mainstream; the ostracized communities were tolerated but not wholly accepted. Invading Europeans considered the Native Americans heathens and became determined to instill Western culture, religion, and social mores. Native Americans were conquered, not accepted. The forced coexistence did not lead to a functioning or healthy society.

When different cultures coexist with acceptance there is no dominate, superior, or guiding culture. There is no one culture in the center focus or at the top. When cultures are accepting of each other's mores without hierarchical comparison, multiculturalism flourishes and society benefits.

America is a multicultural society. The marginalization of ethnicities and their cultures remains an historical fact. The lack of acceptance has had detrimental effects causing people, specifically health professionals, to think in hierarchical comparisons. This mistake cannot continue through the actions of health professionals. We must cease hierarchical thinking, European-centered thinking, with all patients. The question becomes—can European-centered thinking be altered? The answer is to develop a culturally competent way of thinking to assure European culture does not permanently remain the center focus.

In order to understand the term culture, necessary to understand what is being forced into one's center focus, a learner must first be familiar with the terms race and ethnicity.

Race:

Race can be defined from a biological and sociological perspective. The biological concept of race has been long divided into five criteria.[7]

1. The biological foundation generates discrete racial groupings such that all members of one race share a set of biological characteristics that are not shared by members of other races.

2. This biological foundation is inherited from one generation to the next generation, allowing observers to identify an individual race through their ancestry or genetics.

3. Genealogical investigations should identify each race's geographic origin, typically Africa, Europe, Asia, or North America and South America.

---

7   "Race," *Stanford Encyclopedia of Philosophy Archive*, (Spring 2018): https://plato.stanford.edu/archives/spr2017/entries/race/

Elisa P. Bell, M.D.

4. This inherited racial biological foundation manifests itself primarily in physical phenotypes, such as skin color, eye color, hair texture, and bone structure, and perhaps behavioral phenotypes.

Race simply describes a person's birth origin, physical characteristics, and behavioral phenotype with some biological foundation.

Sociologists define race as a social construct to describe how people think and treat groups of people. They believe this was an idea that was created to justify inequality. The term race did not exist before the sixteenth century. Race is a modern concept developed in the sixteenth century by Europeans who divided people into several groups such as Caucasoid, Mongoloid, and Negroid.[8]

In ancient times, people were divided by their religion, language, lineage, and nationality rather than by physical appearance. Later, the concept of race was used to justify inequality and colonization.

On June 26, 2000, President Bill Clinton with Francis Collins, M.D., Ph.D., gave a press conference about the results of a fifteen-year endeavor called *The Human Genome Project*. Dr. Collins, the Director of NIMH/Genetics Department, successfully completed a complex multidisciplinary scientific interpretation, discovering, mapping and sequencing human DNA. He said at the press conference that all humans are 99.9% identical and of that .1% difference, 94% of the variations is among individuals from the same population, and the other 6% between individuals from different populations. He said, "We are all one race, the human race."

Ethnicity:

Ethnicity is defined as belonging to a social group, and either identifies with or is identified by others as a mix of cultural and other

---

8   Ibid

factors including language, diet, religion, ancestry, and physical features associated with race. The social definition of ethnicity refers to one's cultural background, or geographical origin. An ethnicity is a population group whose members identify with each other on the basis of common nationality. It denotes a shared group history. Often, ethnicity is a choice. If people believe they descend from a particular group, and they want to be associated with that group, then they are in fact members of that group.[9]

Differences between race and ethnicity:

Race is determined by physical characteristics and appearance, whereas ethnicity is often a chosen social group to which one belongs. A person can have more than one ethnicity. A young woman born and raised in East Africa, Kenya, until the age of eleven, is adopted by a French family. She has become acculturated in East Africa as well as France (learned the language, diet, religion, and culture). She is identified racially by her inherited Kenyan biological makeup: skin color, eye color, bone structure, and hair texture, but she shares the ethnicity of Kenya and France. Ethnically, she is both Kenyan and French.[10]

During the late 1800s and early 1900s, the "one-drop rule" classified people as African American. The rule dictated that if a person had one drop of African blood the person was African American. To be classified as such meant a loss of civil rights and liberties. This denial of rights led many African Americans who appeared white to live as white and deny their African American ethnicity, to "pass." These people looked white—but were African American by definition of the one-drop rule. This rule originated in the southern states of America, and ultimately swept the nation.

---

9 "Ethnicity vs. Race," *Diffen.com*, (n.d.): https://www.diffen.com/difference/Ethnicity_vs_Race
10 Ibid

Elisa P. Bell, M.D.

By 1960, Americans were able to choose their race on the census. Finally, in the year 2000, the US Census Bureau changed its standard of classification of federal data pertaining to race and ethnicity. Race and ethnicity were reported as distinct identities. Americans were allowed to choose more than one racial category to identify themselves.

In 2013, the US Census Bureau reported that nine million Americans choose two or more racial categories when asked about their race. According to Pew social trends, approximately 6.9% of the US population can be considered multiracial. Multiracial adults cannot be easily categorized.

The majority of multiracial adults with a mixed ancestry of African and European closely align themselves with the African American race; census information tells us approximately 69% of multiracial Americans consider their experiences, attitudes, and social interactions to be African American-based. Multiracial adults from different races, for example white and Indian, and white and Asian, closely align themselves with the majority white race. In America, 66% of multiracial Latinos identify with their Hispanic background. Hispanic origin is treated as an ethnicity rather than a race.

Multiracial Hispanics often say they are Hispanic with two separate races. This is consistent with the US Census Bureau in counting mixed-race Hispanics. The United States Census Bureau predicts that by the year 2069, 66-70% of America will be non-white.

Culture:

Culture is defined as a set of customs, traditions, and values of a society or community such as an ethnic group or nation. It is the social behavior and norms found in human societies. Chamberlin defines culture as the values, norms, traditions that affect how an individual of a particular group perceives, thinks, interacts, behaves, and makes judgments about their world.[11] Researches from Texas A&M take a closer look at the term:

1. Culture refers to the cumulative deposit of knowledge, experience, symbolic community, beliefs, values, attitudes, meaning communication, hierarchies, religion, notion of time, roles, spatial relations, concepts of the universe, and material objects and possessions acquired by a group of people in the course of generations through individual and group skills.

2. Culture is community, and community is culture.

3. Culture is, in its broader sense, behavioral in that it is the totality of each person's learned and accumulated experiences, which is socially transmitted through behavior and social learning.[12]

Everyone has a culture. Some individuals may not understand their culture, possibly because in America there is a lack of awareness about culture and how it influences one's daily life. Culture is a system of shared meanings. People who are placed either by census categories or through self-identification, regardless of race and ethnic group, are often assumed to share the same culture. This is an overgeneralization because not all group members in a given racial category share the same culture identity.

Cultural identity refers to the culture that someone identifies with; one in which the person has shared beliefs and patterns. All humans are cultural beings. Culture is not just simply race and ethnicity. Culture is constantly changing because shifts in societal beliefs and environmental demands influence culture.

---

11   Steven Chambers, "Recognizing and Responding to Cultural Differences in Education of Culturally and Linguistically Diverse Leaners," *Intervention in School and Clinic,* (March 2005): https://journals.sagepub.com/doi/10.1177/10534512050400040101

12   "Culture," *People Texas A&M.* (n.d.): http://people.tamu.edu/~i-choudhury/culture.html

Acculturation refers to a socialization process by which minority and immigrant groups gradually adopt selective elements from a dominant culture. The American culture is transformed by the interaction with minority and immigrant groups. These interactions become more complex because minority and immigrant groups form a culture distinct from both their country of origin and the dominant culture of America. Ignoring, not recognizing, generalizing, or not being aware of these cultural interactions is a lack of cultural competency. Many people consider themselves to have multicultural identities.

Intersectionality:

The term intersectionality is a term that was first coined by American civil rights advocate Kimberlé Williams Crenshaw. It is the theory of multidimensional oppression. Intersectionality is the idea that multiple identities intersect to create a whole that is different from the component identities. Examples of these identities include, in part: religion, age, race, gender, sexual orientation, ethnicity, social class, as well as physical and mental disability. The belief is that these identities are intersecting and link together to comprise one's identity. Intersectionality is key and critical when discussing multicultural identities.

Often, there is such a strong focus on a specific racial or ethnic population, that no one is taking a closer look at an individual being gay, disabled, poor, or illiterate. Yet, these cultural components are all intersecting, and must be taken into consideration by a health professional.

Cultural competency:

A culturally competent health profession is constantly in pursuit of cultural information concerning patients. Cultural competency recognizes cultures as equal and relevant to a patient's health. Cultural competence engages in thorough ongoing self-examination, including being mindful of prejudiced cultural thoughts and awareness of unconscious racial hierarchy. This self-examination is rooted in a deep exploration of how one's culture impacts their mindset, beliefs, and actions toward people that are culturally different from them. Cultural competence requires that cultural assumptions and stereotypes be quickly identified and recognized as problems in thought that might affect the behavior of the health professional. Intersectionality must be understood for each individual, and the cultural interactions that occur between different cultures cannot be ignored or considered unimportant. Western culture must not remain the center focus for every patient. A health provider improving in culturally competency seeks the ability and the knowledgeable assistance to place each patient's culture at center focus.

Chapter Two

Why Cultural Competency?

The Hippocratic Oath states, "I will use treatment to help the sick according to my ability and judgment, but never with a view to injury and wrongdoing." A health professional cannot heal with limited cultural knowledge of a patient, and the lack of knowledge causes harm.

Not understanding a patient's culture, not improving cultural competency becomes problematic. There is great diversity among cultural groups. Therefore, a clinician and practitioner cannot know all about the subgroups within a particular group, but the practitioner should learn how to obtain and gather information about particular cultures and groups in each case.[13] The lack of cultural competency among America's healthcare professionals leads to several problems: patient dissatisfaction and ostracism, over- and under-medicating, language and communication barriers, adherence to treatment, misdiagnosis, and unequal treatment and care-based racial hierarchy.

When a health professional treats a patient as if they are only an ailment or their reason for seeking help is their own fault, the patient feels it. For example, a pregnant middle-aged Mexican woman comes

---

13   Terry L. Cross et al., "Towards a Culturally Competent System of Care," *CASSP*, (March 1989): https://files.eric.ed.gov/fulltext/ED330171.pdf

into emergency thinking her water has broken. A doctor examines her and determines the baby has shifted and applied pressure to her bladder. The doctor responds that she should have known the difference between a baby making her urinate and her water breaking.

The doctor may have assumed the pregnant patient was an experienced mother due to her age and her race; his comments and assumptions illustrate a lack of cultural competence. His statements could easily cause the patient to be dissatisfied with the facility and feel as if the doctor were racist. High patient dissatisfaction and strong feelings of ostracism are byproducts of health professionals who lack cultural competence.

A provider with culturally competent knowledge will not make assumptions and will avoid commenting on stereotypical beliefs; with proper training, even unconscious stereotypical beliefs and statements can be curtailed; both of these errors can be reduced to lessen patient dissatisfaction and feelings of ostracism.

Another unfortunate byproduct that results from a lack of cultural competency is over- and under-medicating. If a doctor limits the amount of pain medication prescribed to a young Puerto Rican, due to believing that Puerto Ricans sell their pain medication, the patient suffers from the physician's lack of cultural competency. When a middle-aged African American female patient is diagnosed with diabetes, and a physician decides to also prescribe high blood pressure medicine based on the patient's age and race, the assumption that because the patient is African American, high blood pressure is a certainty, also indicates a lack in cultural competency. Not all middle-aged African Americans have hypertension. When a heath professional's stereotypical beliefs and assumptions interfere with them seeing the patient as a unique individual, that professional lacks cultural competency.

Often, language and communication barriers cause health providers to jump to conclusions. An inability to communicate well in English does not indicate illiteracy or poor mental capacity. Polish Americans, Mexican Americans, Jamaican Americans, and Chinese Americans have all struggled with and suffered from the assumption that language proficiency (in English) indicates intelligence; this error also reflects an absence of cultural competency. In the US, 37 million Americans speak languages other than English, with almost half of these Americans speaking English "less than very well." Their lack of mastery in English does not diminish their intelligence. Many Polish Americans often speak Russian. Many Jamaican Americans speak French and Spanish. To judge intelligence by English proficiency posits racial hierarchy, again, placing Europe as the center focus. When health professionals believe that European culture is superior to other cultures, diminished cultural competency is obvious.

People, patients, know when they are being belittled, and this often results in failure to adhere to treatment. Trust is the major factor in relationships between healthcare professionals and patients. If a patient doesn't trust that the healthcare provider supports and understands their interests, they will not follow the provider's suggestions and directives. Patients don't appreciate being viewed as "a lesser." Provider directives given as if one is talking to a child do not build trust among adults. Limited trust yields limited adherence. A health professional with cultural competency will garner much more compliance from patients.

It is absurd to expect every heath professional to enjoy complete knowledge about all cultures. What is expected is open-mindedness to cultural differences without hierarchy, and consideration in treatment.

Belief in spirits and talking to and seeking guidance from deceased ancestors, or believing that trees and other plants have consciousness, or studying crystals for their healing ability, are not reasons to diagnose one with mental health issues. These are cultural differences, and not understanding that leads to misdiagnosis. An absence of cultural competency often bears fruit in the misdiagnoses of children. Children from different cultural backgrounds behave differently. To expect all children to fit into a single mold leads to many children being misdiagnosed with behavioral problems.

Our nation suffers from racial hierarchy and European-centered thought. These trends promote behaviors devaluing other cultures. These problems surface when patients receive unequal treatment and unequal care based on hierarchical racial thinking, resulting in patient dissatisfaction and ostracism. It begets over- and under-medicating, language and communication barriers, failures to follow treatment, and misdiagnosis. To correct this, providers of all stripes must value other cultures. European culture should never be permanently center focus for every patient. Cultural competency comes into play by teaching health professionals to recognize when they are operating from a European-centered focus, and when they are denying the recognition of a patient's culture during treatment.

Chapter Three
Improving Cultural Competency

Before improving one's cultural competency, it must first be understood that cultural competency is a process, not just an obtainable state. Cultural competence is a continuous lifelong learning process. Terry Cross writes:

Cultural competence is a set of congruent behaviors, attitudes, and policies that come together in a system, agency, or among professionals and enable that system, agency, or those professionals to work effectively in cross-cultural situations. The word "culture" is used because it implies the integrated pattern of human behavior that includes thoughts, communications, actions, customs, beliefs, values, and institutions of a racial, ethnic, religious, or social group. The word competence is used because it implies having the capacity to function effectively. A culturally competent system of care acknowledges and incorporates—at all levels—the importance of culture, the assessment of cross-cultural relations, vigilance towards the dynamics that result from cultural differences, the expansion of cultural knowledge, and the adaptation of services to meet culturally-unique needs.[14]

---

14   Ibid

Cross ends the discussion with culture because it is dynamic. Each practitioner, organization, and system carry with them their own cultural history which influence each entity's (clinic, each hospital, and every practitioner) cultural competency training.[15]

There are many cultural competence (CC) training models throughout the US. However, there is no standardized training course for healthcare professionals to follow, and this is a point of contention for scholars. Watt discusses the lack of empirical evidence on the impact of CC on patient outcomes. Watt writes that what patients deem as "clinically safe" should be examined; therefore, there should be an assessment of CC practitioners from the patient's perspective.[16]

In support of CC training, Alizadeah and Chavan offer positive outcomes from CC training:

1. Increased numbers of patients seeking treatment

2. Lower rates of morbidity and mortality

3. Increased adherence to treatment

4. Higher level of trust

5. Increased feelings of self-esteem

6. Improved health status

7. Greater satisfaction with care[17]

Further support for the needed CC training comes from the National Center for Cultural Competency. The center argues that CC training helps to respond to current and projected demographic changes in the US:

---

15   Wyatt et al., "Developing CC in General Practitioners and Integral review of Literature," *BMC FAM PRACT* 17, no.1 (2016):158.

16   Somayeh Alizadeh and Meena Chavan, "Culture Competent Dimensions and Outcome: A Systems Review of the Literature," *Health Social Care Community*:24 no.6 (October 2016) 117-130: https://onlinelibrary.wiley.com/doi/full/10.1111/hsc.12293.

17   For more review of the items visit: https://nccc.georgetown.edu

1. To eliminate the healthcare disparity gap of people of diverse, ethnic, and racial/cultural backgrounds

2. To improve the quality of service and healthcare outcomes

3. To meet legislative, regulatory, and accreditation mandates

4. To gain a competitive edge in the marketplace

5. To decrease the likelihood of liability and malpractice claims[18]

Several challenges get in the way of starting a CC training class. The first challenge: creating an environment receptive to receiving and acknowledging the need for CC training. To establish a conducive environment, some institutions and organizations use online training courses, provide training on site, and suggest an ongoing year-to-year continuum. Cross discusses six steps for establishing continuous CC training.[19]

A second challenge: learner resistance. Learning alters one's frame of reference, and this often meets resistance. Resistance means to defy, to not take part in the experience.[20] Several years ago while giving a lecture on CC to a group of medical professionals, I encountered several practitioners before the lecture resistant to complete a self-assessment IQ test on CC. I showed them that the process of becoming more CC is to assess oneself, to see "where you are on the continuum." I also said the self-scoring information was in their packets and informed them that no one would see their score. I still met resistance.

They challenged why I chose this particular CC IQ exam. Several practitioners displayed anger, anxiety, and stress over answering CC IQ questions. To counter these concerns, I discussed ethnocentrism, including the thought, "our way is the only way and the right way." I

---

18   Terry L. Cross et al., "Towards a Culturally Competent System of Care," *CASSP,* (March 1989): https://files.eric.ed.gov/fulltext/ED330171.pdf

19   Ibid

20   Ibid

assured them that no one was trying to take away their culture or trying to diminish who they were by becoming aware of another's culture. I reiterated that we all must look at ourselves, and what makes us who we are to better embrace cultural competency.

I told them that we have all been influenced by our families, our politics, our religion, our media, our peers, our teachers, our communication style, our physical environment, our race, our ethnicity, and our beliefs and values. I wanted them to understand how important it is to identify our influencers through self-assessment. Fortunately, this discussion allowed the training to continue.

The word humility appears frequently in CC literature. Practitioners, trainers and coaches must practice humility in CC training. Humility is a concept, not a technique, but learning to be humble is also a process and critical goal in CC communication. One must practice humbleness.[21] Clinicians who are the most successful are the ones who practice humility, as they see themselves as becoming rather than being culturally competent.[22]

Cultural competency is a lifelong process. Practitioners, organizations, and systems are at different levels of awareness and knowledge along the CC continuum. Before training, a self-assessment helps know where each clinician or organization falls on the CC continuum. The National Center on Cultural Competency lists Cultural Competency Assessments on its website.[23]

There are multiple CC training modules in the literature. The most complete model with more than a textbook approach featuring

---

21   E-shien Chang et al., "Integrating Culture Humility Into Healthcare Professionals Education and Training," *Advances in Health Sciences Education,* 17, no. 2 (May 2012): 269–278, https://link.springer.com/article/10.1007/s10459-010-9264-1
22   Ibid
23   "The mission of the NCCC is to increase the capacity of healthcare and mental healthcare programs to design, implement, and evaluate culturally and linguistically competent service delivery systems to address growing diversity, persistent disparities, and to promote health and mental health equity" see - https://nccc.georgetown.edu.

Elisa P. Bell, M.D.

"how to" step-by-step guide is from Terry L. Cross.[24] The Cross model emphasizes the framework for Cultural competency, along a phased continuum:

1. Cultural Destructiveness

2. Cultural Incapacity

3. Cultural Blindness

4. Cultural Pre-Competence

5. Cultural Competency

6. Cultural Proficiency.[25]

The National Center of Cultural Competency at Georgetown modified the Cross model as follows:

1. Have a defined set of values and principles, and demonstrate behaviors, attitudes, policies, and structures that enable them to work effectively cross-culturally.

2. Have the capacity to a. value diversity, b. conduct self-assessments, c. manage the dynamics of difference, d. acquire and institutionalize cultural knowledge, and f. adapt to diversity and the cultural contexts of communities they serve.

References

"Six Steps Towards Cultural Competency: A Clinicians Guide"Home Healthcare Management and Practice 14(5): 378—386.

Website https://nccc.georgetown.edu/assessments or University of Michigan website at http://www.med.umich.edu/multicultural/

National Center of Cultural Competency at Georgetown University https://nccc.georgetown.edu

---

24   Terry L. Cross et al., "Towards a Culturally Competent System of Care," *CASSP*, (March 1989): https://files.eric.ed.gov/fulltext/ED330171.pdf

25   Ibid

Chapter Four

Case Reflections

From these cases, readers should see the positive differences culturally competent health providers contribute to a patient's life and society. Our need to improve cultural competence remains urgent; so many have suffered enough.

Please note: each scholar chose their own academic writing style for their article.

Morris A. Blount, Jr., M.D.

Adult Psychiatrist

Psychiatric Treatment of Latina Transgendered Female

AB is a twenty-three-year-old (transgendered) female of Mexican descent, first seen by this writer in 2012 when she was transferred from the Child Psychiatry Department at the Community Mental Health Center where this writer is employed. At the time, she was diagnosed with depression. Currently, the diagnoses are PTSD, bipolar II disorder, and gender dysphoria, post-transition. She has a history of self-mutilation via cutting her arms and legs, and she has had one suicide attempt via overdose as an adolescent. Latina adolescents have the highest rate of suicidal ideation and attempts of any ethnic and gender group in this age. (Kramer et al. 2009) AB has been on several medications, including: Clonidine, Fluoxetine, Mirtazapine, Venlafaxine XR, Lurasidone, Aripiprazole, and Quetiapine. She is currently taking Risperidone, Chlorpromazine, and Citalopram. She has been hospitalized three times, first at the age of seventeen and most recently at the age of twenty, with the most recent hospitalization occurring after an argument with her father. She does not have a history of alcohol or drug abuse and does not have current medical problems. She is taking hormones for the trans-gendering process. There is a history of depression and anxiety in her mother's family.

She is from Chicago and the youngest of five siblings. She describes a history of physical and emotional abuse from her father and being emotionally abused by peers growing up, calling her derogatory names, such as "*joto* and faggot" due to not being "boy enough." She dropped out of school during the twelfth grade and is contemplating a General Education Diploma (GED). She has had a history of numerous relationships with older men, who reportedly initially claim to want to take care of her. The relationships have not lasted long, and the patient goes through periods of anger, rage, and sadness when the relationships end. She has not had any jobs, currently lives with her mother and father.

There have not been medication changes in over a year and the patient has worked in psychotherapy (with another provider) on coping with day-to-day interactions with others as well as on how she is perceived, especially now that her appearance has changed due to hormonal therapy.

Working with this patient, the cultural issues that have arisen relate to the following: general mental health treatment and the Latina patient, LGBT issues in mental health treatment, and LGBT issues with the Latina patient.

Specific to this patient have been matters of:

- Not having familial support for psychiatric treatment
- How her father's heavy drinking and violent tendencies seem to have been accepted, but her psychiatric diagnoses have not
- Not being "masculine enough" in a Latino culture
- Having people confuse gender dysphoria with being a crossdresser
- Not being taken seriously when first expressing gender dysphoria
- Feeling alone and somewhat marginalized, even within the lesbian-gay-bisexual-transgender (LGBT) community
- Upon review of the APA best practices and guidelines when working with LGBTQ and Latino populations (2005), principals that have been pertinent in providing services to AB have been to:

- Use a bio-psycho-social-cultural model of evaluation and treatment

- Take the time to develop a cultural formulation

- Support collaborative care

- Recognize that gender and sexuality continuums are separate, yet interrelated realms.

- Be aware that the gender continuum breaks down into separate, but not mutually exclusive, masculine and feminine continuums.

- Realize that sexuality is composed of three distinct realms: orientation and attraction, behavior, and identity. These three realms are interrelated, but not always aligned.

- Know that gender may develop based upon biologic sex, but this is not always the case (i.e., transgendered, intersex, androgynous individuals).

According to the 2001 *Supplement to the Surgeon General's Report Mental Health: Culture, Race, and Ethnicity,* stigma is a pervasive problem preventing members of all racial and ethnic minority groups from seeking behavioral health care for mental disorders including substance use. Stigma is a particularly critical problem among members of Latino ethnic groups. (Kramer et al. 2009). This patient reported that when she first began to have noticeable mood fluctuations, they were attributed to her stressful home environment. The familial explanation was *nervios*. She describes that the symptoms were perceived to be "just a reaction to everything going on at home and problems at school."

Kramer et al. (2009) states that *nervios* is referring to an individual's general state of vulnerability to stress and to a syndrome of symptoms triggered by stress. Symptoms of *nervios* include headaches, irritability, stomach disturbances, trembling, and dizziness. *Nervios* captures a spectrum, which can range from being sensitive to stress *padecer de nervios* to other presentations that may include adjustment, anxiety, depressive, dissociative, somatoform or psychotic disorders (APA 2005; Guarnaccia et al 2003).

As time progressed and AB's symptoms worsened, a hospitalization was required following an overdose and mood-stabilizing medications were initiated. This was particularly distressing to the patient as she, having then been prescribed "hard core" medications, was then labeled *loco*, which she said was more embarrassing. (Prior to that time, pharmacotherapy consisted of Clonidine for "my being hyper.") She has stated that her mother was receptive to her being prescribed Clonidine, especially since it is also an antihypertensive; she was not as willing for the patient to start antidepressant therapy, despite her own symptomatology.

According to Kramer et al. (2009), in many Latino cultures, a person is labeled as *loco* if he or she has to take medications to control his or her symptoms and behavior. According to the DSM-IV-TR Glossary of Culture-Bound Syndromes, *Locura* is "A term used by Latinos in the United States and Latin America to refer to a severe form of chronic psychosis." Once one is labeled as suffering from *locura*, it is very difficult to recover or to lose the label of loco. Furthermore, needing to take medications is seen as a sign of weakness or laziness and indicates that the person is not working hard enough to get well. If the person's efforts to get better fail, there is a fear that the illness may be incurable and that the person has crossed over into *locura* (Lu et al 2006).

This patient found the transgender issue more complicated, as she herself had to discern sexual attraction to men from gender dysphoria. She was teased as a child, for "wanting to do girly things" and later, as an adolescent, for "not being masculine enough" and "not wanting to chase after girls (for sex)." As she felt distanced from adolescent males, she gravitated toward females and "wanted big boobs like some girls got." She did develop female friends and was actually seen as non-threatening by their boyfriends; however, some of the females also shunned her when she expressed that "I am really a girl, too … they thought I was a freak." She then learned that her desire to do things that were societally feminine were attributed to being "just a faggot," and was also called *joto*, (a colloquial derogatory term for gay males). Also, she was told that the gender dysphoria was "just made up … you just don't want to admit that you are a faggot." She could not label her gender dysphoria, but just felt that "I was not really a guy." She felt that "I just did not fit in." It was during that time that she attempted suicide via overdose.

This patient's experiences are apparently not unusual. The 2008 National Center for Transgender Equality (NCTE) and the National Gay and Lesbian Task Force had results to showed that forty-seven percent of Latinos/respondents reported having attempted suicide, compared to forty-one percent of all study respondents and one-point-six percent of the general U.S. population. This same survey found that seventy-seven percent of Latinos/respondents who attended school experienced some form of harassment.

Having AB as a patient has been a learning experience for this writer, as I have appreciated her openness with me and her willingness to educate me, especially regarding Spanish terms as they relate to her psychiatric history and details about the trans-gendering process. Regarding my own experiences in becoming more culturally competent, most of the impetus for learning has come from my life trajectory. Growing up in a primarily African-American, Southern (US), Protestant, heterosexual and politically left-leaning environment, moving to a metropolis exposed me to individuals who have had completely different life experiences. And, practicing in the urban environment that exists in Chicago has exposed me to a diverse patient population; it would not be clinically sound to ignore the importance of cultural competence.

To enhance my knowledge as it relates to cultural competence, I usually make an effort to read related articles that appear in professional periodicals. Also, attending professional conferences that have cultural awareness seminars/lectures has been beneficial. Most importantly, however, has been the opportunity to discuss culturally competent issues with not only patients, who appreciate the respectful inquisitiveness, but with colleagues with whom I work, who also welcome the opportunity for dialogue.

References

American Psychiatric Association (APA). (2005). Practice Guideline for the Psychiatric

Evaluation of Adults. Washington, DC: American Psychiatric Association (APA)

Grant, J., Mottet, L., Tanis, J., Harrison, J.; L. Herman, L., Keiling, M. Injustice at Every Turn, A Report of the National Transgender Survey, 2008

Guarnaccia, P.J., R. Lewis-Fernandez and M. Rivera Marano. 2003. Toward a Puerto Rican popular nosology: *Nervios* and *Ataques de Nervios*. Culture, Medicine and Psychiatry 27:339-366

Kramer, E.; Guarnaccia, P.; Resendez, C.; Lu, F.; Barreras, B; Brainin-Rodriguez, J. No Soy Loco!/I'm Not Crazy, Understanding the Stigma of Mental Illness in Latinos Jan 1, 2009

Lu FG (2006): DSM-IV Outline for Cultural Formulation: Bringing Culture into the Clinical

Encounter. FOCUS. IV (1). 9-10

U.S. Department of Health and Human Services. 2001. Mental Health: Culture, Race, and Ethnicity. Rockville, MD: U.S. Department of Health and Human Services, Public Health Service, Office of the Surgeon General

Lynne Mock, PhD.

Research Manager Center for Community Corrections Research

Illinois Criminal Justice Information Authority

Training for Cultural Competency in Psychiatry

Cultural competency in psychiatry gives effective and efficient mental health care to a diverse population with differences in the areas of gender, race, ethnicity, sexual orientation, age, religion, ability/disability, language/bilingual/multilingual, national origin, immigration status, socioeconomic status, and any relevant subcultures in which their patient is immersed or inspiring to connect (Bassey, 2013).

Culture involves human behavioral and attitudinal patterns involving thoughts, communications, actions, values, customs, beliefs, values, and institutions of a specific group that may be defined by nationality, race, ethnicity, religion, profession, or any other social group. Competence refers to having the requisite knowledge, skill, and capacity to be effective in an endeavor. Cultural competency refers to a set of policies, attitudes, and behaviors that are systematically applied to ensure that an individual can function in cross-cultural situations and be aware of the impact of one's own culture in professional practice (Bassey, 2013).

Psychiatry cannot ignore social context. Cultural values dictate scientific priorities, politics dictates diagnoses, and an increasingly corporate culture in psychiatry uses performance-based outcomes in under-resourced environments with decreased government expenditures for the medically indigent. There are greater managed-care restrictions on types and lengths of treatment, resulting in less inpatient care and fifteen-minute outpatient medication appointments. The profession and their insurers favor pharmacotherapy over psychotherapy when both could be more effective (Aggarwal, 2015).

As a demographic, psychiatrists in leadership are more likely to be older, white men than women or racially diverse people of color. The organizational cultural competence of psychiatrists remains unexamined. It is unclear the level of cultural competency taught in medical schools, or practiced in hospitals, or provider networks. However, psychiatrists who wish to learn more about culture and its impact on their practice have several resources available through the American Psychiatric Association.

While the profession of psychiatry has created cultural competency standards and evaluation outcomes, how often are the standards assessed and met? Psychiatrists must be or become aware of important areas of knowledge and skill development for a culturally competent practice, such as social distance (class), gender, and race (Aggarwal, 2015).

Psychiatry trainees, and those going through licensing updates, should be assessed for cultural competency and receive recommendations for knowledge skill development tailored to their demonstrated strengths and weaknesses (Aggarwal, 2013). Researchers who study cultural competency for psychiatrists recommend avoiding assumptions of cultural incompetence and avoiding the need for self-examination and self-disclosures about biases between the psychiatrist and their patient. Students were averse to self-reflection and self-criticism about their own cultural backgrounds in relationship to their differences from individual patients' racial, ethnic, linguistic, and socio-economic background (Aggarwal, 2013).

What is more productive is to have psychiatrists and those in training to conduct some self-reflection on their own attitudes and biases that may impact their clinical practice. These issues can be explored in supervision, rather than in a classroom or clinic setting. Researchers found that trainees appreciated an approach that avoided stereotyping patients and developing a strong knowledge base in various cultures and subcultures. Instead, psychiatric trainees preferred to be involved in several different types of cultural competency learning experiences. They appreciated discussion of their own acculturation process within medicine and psychiatry. They wanted to learn how to address cross-cultural miscommunication. Also, they wanted to understand the relevance of cultural competency to formulating and implementing care for actual patient in case studies (Aggarwal, 2013). Actual case studies can be useful to guide self-refection on how their own attitudes and biases may impact their patients and overall clinical practice.

However, some researchers and psychiatrists are concerned that cultural competency may be elusive given the diversity of our human family. Culturally competent practice in psychiatry must move beyond a superficial understand of different cultures. For example, for African Americans, within group diversity, within-group differences, and various contexts within which individuals exist. Learning and working with the patient's communication style, worldview, level of assimilation/acculturation, and beliefs about mental health are important factors in culturally competent care (Bassey, 2013).

According to Bassey (2013) there are several important components of cultural competence:

1. *Awareness* - a process of acknowledging cultural difference and its importance. For instance, culture influences goals, and how people attempt to meet their needs. In sessions with clients, the psychiatrist must be aware of how the patients may influence goal setting and prioritizing needs and wants.

2. *Critical self-awareness* - the psychiatrist would build awareness of their own culturally influenced perspective (which should be discussed in supervision as early as possible), self-scrutiny and self-reflection must be ongoing for professional growth and development. Questioning one's own assumptions is key, as well as scanning the socio-cultural environments surrounding one's therapeutic practice. Examining one's own personal reactions to race, gender, and how this may impact clinical practice.

3. *Identity* – it must be understood that *identity has many dimensions and intersections*. What identity is most salient to the client? It may not be the difference in which the psychiatrist is most aware. Allow the patient to discuss and reveal what part of their identity is salient and relevant to the therapeutic goals. Cultural identity researchers have looked at racial/ethnic identity; feminist/womanist identity, biracial identity, disability identity, LGBTQ identities, and levels of acculturation for minorities within a larger and different majority culture. However, understanding is important but not sufficient. It is critical for psychiatrists to be non-judgmental while learning their patient's cultural background, values, beliefs, priorities, and worldview.

4. *Knowledge* – is knowing the characteristics and complexities of a patient's specific cultural groups. Knowledge should support the formation of the therapeutic alliance, trust, safety, support, and rapport in a therapeutic relationship. It is necessary to learn and understand beliefs about mental health; mental illness; and beliefs about mind, body, and spirit that may overlap in the religious/spiritual realm—which many believe influences their behaviors and outcomes. It is important to learn about family systems, help-seeking behavior, traditions, and the history of a patient's culture.

5. *Skills* – being able to understand the communication and language patterns of one's patients, including non-verbal behaviors, expressiveness (volume, tone pitch, sighs, silence), interpreters, denotation and connotation of language. Communication is very important in the process of building the therapeutic relationship. During communication, credibility is key, and influences patients' motivation for therapy and expectations for success.

6. *Empathic understanding* - is necessary as a means to avoid stereotypes but still acknowledge the patient's important cultural factors. Through dialogue, the psychiatrist should reach a shared understanding of the patient's experiences, issues, and goals, and allow these conversations to influence therapeutic intervention strategies and goals.

Sperry theorized that cultural approaches to psychiatry have four distinct dimensions, and some see these dimensions as an orderly progression of increasing cultural awareness and competency. The first dimension is *Cultural Awareness*, using cultural knowledge to recognize cultural problems or issues for a specific patient and their situation. The second dimension is *Cultural Sensitivity*, the capacity to identify cultural problems or issues and respond empathically and without judgment. The third dimension is *Cultural Competence*, the ability to draw upon cultural knowledge and skillful actions to work effectively with patients of different cultural backgrounds. Acceptance, cooperation, tolerance, collaboration, and mutuality are essential behaviors to demonstrate in the therapeutic relationship. And the last is *Cultural Action*, translating cultural sensitivity into the psychiatrists' and the patients' behaviors, in which the psychiatrist learns to make healthy decisions on behalf of their patients, and respond skillfully to the needs of the patients within their cultural sphere (Sperry, 2013).

Fisher-Borne (2015) posits that *Cultural Humility* is an attainable alternative to cultural competence. Criticism of cultural competency suggests that the focus on comfort with "others" via self-awareness may not be effective, and where is the evidence to support this process? Critics also propose that culture obscures racial/ethnic group identity, indeed there is much diversity within cultures that is important to illuminate and explore. Some are concerned that the emphasis on obtaining cultural knowledge to become competent is unattainable and does not take into account the diversity of clientele such that becoming competent in many different cultures can be a difficult accomplishment. Also, cultures are fluent and ever-changing, and that outdated cultural knowledge can become restrictive, and in some situations, unhealthy.

Last, in reality, and given the constraints of the training and the profession of psychiatry, the lack of cultural action, the psychiatrist's ability to be involved in transformative social justice agendas to address and challenge social inequalities, is a reality with very serious consequences to patients and their communities, but the skills and knowledge to enact cultural action can be elusive (Fisher-Borne, 2015).

Instead, Fisher-Borne (2015) suggests that *Cultural Humility*— committing to ongoing relationships with patients, communities, and colleagues that requires humbleness, self-reflection, and self-critique—is an alternative to cultural competence. Those who practice cultural humility acknowledge the fluidity and subjectivity of culture at the individual and institutional levels. This concept supports cultural action to address inequalities. If psychiatric suffering and illnesses can be significantly linked to institutional or political practices, then psychiatrists must be in the forefront of confronting and addressing the unhealthy practices.

Cultural competence emphasizes knowledge acquisition, a process that is integral to the professional culture of psychiatrists. However, cultural humility emphasizes the need for accountability towards individuals and for institutions. Fisher-Borne's concept is relatively new and needs more conceptual and empirical work. Including action, accountability, and addressing social inequities would be an essential component of any future research.

References

Aggarwal, N.K. (2015) Cultural issues in psychiatric administration and leadership. *Psychiatry Quarterly, 86,* 337-342

Aggarwal, N.K. & DeSilva, R. (2013). Developing cultural competency in health care professions: A fresh approach. *Medical Education, 47,* 1143-1144.

Bassey, S. & Melluish, S. (2013). Cultural competency for mental health practitioners: A selective narrative review. *Counseling Psychology Quarterly, 26,* 151-173.

Bell, C.C. (2004). *The Sanity of Survival: Reflections on Community Mental Health.* Chicago, IL: Third World Press.

Fisher-Borne, M., Cain, J.M., & Martin, S.L. (2015). From mastery to accountability: Cultural humility as an alternative to cultural competence. *Social Work Education, 34,* 165-181.

Sperry L. (2012). Cultural competence: A primer. *The Journal of Individual Psychology, 68,* 311-320.

Arnell Brady, MA. CCC-SLP/L

Speech and Language Pathologist

ASHA Fellow

Cultural Competence as a Means of Survival

As a black, African American male born and raised in America, cultural competence has been a form of survival for me throughout most of my life. My development of cultural competence began when I graduated from my ninety-nine percent black elementary school and started attending a high school that was ninety-five percent white and hostile toward blacks. There were 107 blacks in my freshman class, but only seven of us made it to graduation four years later. In order for me to survive in that high school, I had to learn some of the cultural ways of white-Irish Americans, white-German Americans, and white-Polish Americans. My developmentally strong black family's active involvement in the African Methodist Episcopal Church, and my freedom in a secure self-sufficient black community, kept my sanity in check while my blackness was under constant derogatory and degrading attack. I was able to realize early that I did not have to give up my blackness in order to survive high school. I simply had to learn how to accept differences, even negative and ignorant ones in others, and I had to stay focused on the main objective, finishing high school on time.

Going to high school I spoke predominately black English, but coming out of high school, I was fluent and proficient in Standard American English and black English, which today is termed code switching. In high school, I also tried to become fluent and proficient in the Spanish language, but I could not and did not have enough time to overcome my racist, white, female Spanish teacher that appeared to be determined to block my learning because of her cultural incompetence. That lesson in developing cultural competence carried me successfully through an undergraduate program in speech-language pathology at an institution that has only graduated one black, African American male in its entire history. It also carried me successfully through a graduate program in speech-language pathology at an institution that has only graduated two black, African American males in speech-language pathology in the entire history of that institution. Cultural competence enabled me, a black, African American male, to enter the field of speech-language pathology, which is the fourth whitest occupation in America (ninety-six percent white, ninety-four percent white female, and about two percent black). Now cultural competence is helping me to not only survive, but also to thrive in the field of speech-language pathology, where I was recently appointed a Fellow in the American Speech Language Hearing Association. The speech-language pathologist is the recognized expert in oral language.

Oral language is the most distinguishing cultural indicator; that is, the oral language of a human community is what binds it together and separates it from other communities. Cultural competence has allowed me to thrive as a professional in the field of speech-language pathology because speech is the great medium through which human cooperation is brought about. Speech or spoken language is the way in which people in a particular area, country or social group pronounce words which represents concepts that have been shaped by many distinct experiences in the world. Oftentimes, one can quickly distinguish where geographically in the world a person is from by the way they speak a language (native or foreign). We use speech to help us achieve common goals. I learned to code switch effectively and was able to be educated adequately in places where blacks were generally not welcomed and expectations for them achieving were low. We use speech for more than just relieving our feelings and/or airing our views. We use speech to persuade others to do what we want them to do, believe what we want them to believe, and awaken understanding. Speech allows us to have new adventures and new learning that propels us into greater relationships with the external world that heightens our inventions and intentions. A culturally competent speech-language pathologist ensures the most appropriate and adequate clinical services when oral language is in need of development, repair, or enhancement. Cultural competence became a real issue in the field of speech-language pathology when it was realized that many culturally incompetent speech-language pathologists were unable to offer appropriate and/or adequate clinical services because they could not overcome their own cultural limitations.

Cultural incompetence was excessively costly; clients were not able to benefit from services and the field of speech-language pathology was limited in its outreach and effectiveness. They did not have adequate knowledge and understanding of the readily identifiable unique cultural variables (including ability, age, beliefs, ethnicity, experience, gender, identity, education, linguistic background, national origin, race, religion, sexual orientation, and socioeconomic status) that people of diverse backgrounds brought to the helping situation which directly influenced outcomes. Today, cultural competence is critical and a required proficiency in the delivery of appropriate and adequate speech-language pathology services in diverse communities.

Recently, this clinician had four Indonesian seminary students from a non-English-speaking nation request assistance in improving their pronunciation of English in order to increase their English intelligibility and their ability to stay in America. As second-language learners, they wanted to become more effective communicators in an English-dominant environment. Their native spoken language was "Bahasa Manggarai Indonesia," and cultural competence demanded that I accept all the components (phonology, semantics, vocabulary, grammar, and pragmatics) of their native spoken language, and to carefully analyze the interaction between spoken Bahasa Manggarai and spoken English. The analysis of the interaction between spoken Bahasa Manggarai and spoken English revealed a number of similarities and differences. The differences were significant enough to greatly reduce their intelligibility in their efforts to speak English. Cultural competence requires cognitive flexibility in addressing change in speaking an oral language because the speaking mechanism is an unconscious process; that is, spoken language is primarily based upon the sense of feeling or touch and the place and speed of movement of the articulators. In developing intelligible speech, one has to consider the contributions of proprioception, breathing, timing, resonance, prosody, muscle strength and memory, muscle and bone movement, and the coordination of parts. In addition, one must realize that the preponderance of the responsibility for effective communication lies on the speaker. This clinician wanted the process of improving the Indonesian seminary students' pronunciation of English to be a harmonious one. They were motivated and excited to change, and we were working together in a timely and efficient manner towards the goal.

Cultural competence also requires that the clinician value the client/student, and therefore, must comply with the principle of "Best Practices" and offer the most up-to-date technology. So, I offered them the "SmartPalate" technology, which is a device that allows the speaker an opportunity to visually monitor tongue movement in real time. The participant can visually observe their tongue movement in real or delayed time while also hearing and feeling their tongue movement during speech efforts. All four students showed significant progress in their pronunciation of English in fifteen sessions, and they were able to pass an English proficiency speaking test.

Francois Jolie, MSW, LCSW, QMHP

Cultural Competence and its Impact on Treatment

Case Study 1

Carlos is a twenty-six-year-old gay, Latino male of Colombian descent. He was diagnosed with depression in 2010. He was experiencing sadness, worry, passive SI, hypersomnia, difficulty concentrating, difficulty completing tasks, chronic tardiness to work (for assignments and projects), restlessness, and low self-esteem. He has high aspirations with no clear way to achieve them, chronic indecision, lack of organization, and impulsive spending.

Lexapro and Abilify were not working for the client. So, he continued to be sad, anxious, and unable to concentrate. He was given a new medication and learned significant self-esteem and ADHD strategies to the point where his work problems subsided. He was able to reduce marijuana usage and organize his space and life. He found a new job. He was deciding on a new, larger apartment, and was able to walk away from a bad relationship for the first time.

Then, his father became ill and was hospitalized out of state. The client, without hesitation, called his new job and resigned because in one week he would be selling all of his belongings and traveling to be with his father at the hospital. If the client were Anglo or even African American, I would have suggested that other people who are more stable, with less to lose, and with less precarious circumstances, agree to be around-the-clock hospital companions. However, I learned that most Latinos have a strong family value. In cases such as this, the family will be with the patient through the full hospital stay, day and night. They will never leave a family member alone in a hospital. That means that everyone in the family must be available one full day or more to

Elisa P. Bell, M.D.

be with the patient no matter what the cost. I accepted his choice. And, when I did that, he began to tell me how shameful it would be for him if he did not give up everything and move to support his father. He has seen what happens to family members who do not comply. They get shunned and are ridiculed and become outcasts.

Had I suggested that he keep his momentum going and let other people with less to lose step in, it would have damaged the relationship. The client chose to do e-therapy while he transitioned to a new therapist. I am an American descendent of African slaves and not Latino. We got along well despite our cultural and ethnic differences because I understood and was able to recognize cultural norms when they came up. I chose to accept or seek to understand those norms before I dared challenge them.

I believe that my approach was correct because I inquired extensively about other family members that have been in the hospital. Asking what other family members did for a living and what the consequence would be if he chose to pursue his career instead of leaving everything behind to care for his dying father.

By accident, later I ran across an article about an interracial couple, Anglo female and Colombian male. The woman writing the article talked about how difficult it was to live with a Colombian man because his family boundaries were blurred. The wife was uncomfortable with how often the family came over or her husband would ask to give up his time with her to be with them. Then a family member went into the hospital. And, according to the article, the husband left home and lived at the hospital with his sibling that was hospitalized. That was something she could never understand.

Case Study 2

Doug Durbin, a thirty-five-year-old gay male, seeking to marry a twenty-six-year-old gay male, told me that he and his partner were both taking PrEP, Pre-Exposure Prophylaxis. My immediate response was surprise and concern. Doug is depressed. He does not feel sexy. He has gained about twenty pounds since he met Kyle three years ago. Kyle is younger and more fit and a receptive sex partner. Doug is jealous of Kyle, who has a part-time job and has been bringing men to their home for sex, while Doug is working. Doug has asked that some rules be followed; such as, letting the other know who they are having sex with and when. But Doug kept walking in on men he had never met having sex with the man he was planning to marry. I think anyone would have been depressed in this situation.

I could not believe Doug was willing to put up with the openness of the relationship. However, we all know the more you tell someone that the person they love is not right for them, the harder they dig in their heels. So, I knew not to go there. I helped Doug verbalize what he was signing up for. And, I helped him understand that because he has allowed Kyle to remain his romantic partner despite Kyle's refusal to comply with their explicit agreement, it would be improper to ask Kyle to change after marriage because Kyle has not been held accountable in any meaningful way before the marriage, and it would be a breach of their implicit contract.

It may be difficult to respect this kind of arrangement, but the client is always entitled to self-determination. At no time was Doug concerned about any other STI. We worked together for about a year. I was there to listen and reflect back. If I had told him what I was thinking or how he was being used or abused he would have shut down. Making sure the client was willing to accept the consequences of his or his partner's behavior was the main concern, not what I thought about what he was doing.

I lived through the '80s, and according to the Center for Disease Control and other publications, the way to protect yourself against HIV was sexual abstinence, monogamy, or safer sex practices. I attempted to bring up the idea that PrEP is a medication that might have side effects. I needed to know if any of the depressive symptoms could be attributed to this new medication. The client was firm in his belief that there were no side effects to this medication and that he and his partner needed to take this medication to continue their polyamorous lifestyle. I still thought that it was ridiculous and that all they had to do was "play safe" and taking PrEP would not be necessary.

I encountered another gay male who was HIV negative and practiced safe sex "most of the time." His experience helped me with my understanding of why gay men are so invested in taking PrEP. Let's call him Roy. Roy is what is known as a "Top." The top is the active/inserting partner in male-to-male intercourse. Roy had answered an ad on a popular website for sexual encounters. He brought his condoms and confided in me that he said his affirmations about being safe and healthy, affirming his commitment to using the condoms no matter what. He entered the stranger's home and got undressed. When it came time for anal sex, his new bottom (or receptive sex partner) provided Roy with lubricant because Roy did not bring his own. According to Roy, it looked and felt like silicone lubricant. Roy allowed the guy from the ad to use the lube on Roy's condom-covered penis.

After a few minutes of intimacy, Roy noticed that it was feeling more and more pleasurable. He looked down and the condom had been completely disintegrated. When Roy pointed the disintegration out to his receptive partner, the bottom replied, "That's okay, I don't mind if you do me without a condom." Roy felt as if he could not trust this person and left.

After hearing this story, I researched broken condom sex, and learned that many "Top" men sabotage condoms to have "busted condom sex." If you are a receptive partner in the throes of passion or under the influence of drugs or alcohol, you are not going to notice a condom tearing.

I now feel that it is worth the risk to take PrEP because being a receptive anal sex partner can be very risky. People will tell you they are "safe" because they are taking PrEP. But one STI educator stated, "PrEP only protects you if you are the one taking it." PrEP is expensive, and it must be used at the same time every day. How many people can take lunch or breakfast at the same time every day without skipping? Do you want to believe that someone you just met is responsible enough with his medication to keep you from getting sick? I don't suggest it.

I am guilty of thinking, "It's 2016. How did you accidentally become infected with HIV?" I am so embarrassed by my ignorance and condemnation. Married and committed people in relationships get HIV all the time. Condoms break, your "Total Top" has been totally bottoming for someone without protection, substance users sometimes share "dirty needles" and people who test positive today may have the virus incubating in them from a previous encounter and you trust what they say or their doctor's note as if that diagnosis lasts forever.

I no longer look at people who take PrEP as being undisciplined, impulsive people "wanting their cake and eating it too." In some situations, it is mandatory. In others, it just makes the most sense.

Elisa P. Bell, M.D.

Joyce R. Miller, MD.

Adult Psychiatrist

Administrative Sidelines

Entering the field of administration was an area unknown to me. My entire career had been focused on direct patient care. Now, the care of numerous patients is my concern. I must determine the most appropriate way to meet their clinical needs. Cultural competence was not a topic I considered a priority upon taking this position, but in retrospect, it is imperative to understand various cultures to meet the day-to-day needs of the department. Otherwise, you will be standing on the sidelines with the inability to push forward the department's agenda, which for me, was to improve the clinical programming provided to patients in the safest and most effective way.

As an administrator, you may find yourself standing on the sidelines due to unforeseeable distractions, which may be related to one's cultural background. You attend to your day-to-day responsibilities with thoughts of everyone having the same agenda, to improve care. Then, later, you realize that alternative individual agendas are the driving force for the operations of the department.

An administrator's lack of knowledge of cultural differences may thwart productive interactions with staff. The same holds true with other interpersonal relationships, including physician-to-patient, physician-to-staff, and physician-to-physician. It is imperative for an administrator to understand the worldview of other people to effectively lead and address departmental needs and growth.

As a medical director, there was a noted diverse medical staff, which included African Americans, Pakistanis, Asians, as well as Caucasians and persons from India. These professionals came with a myriad of differences including their thoughts on gender roles and work rules.

The professionals on staff possessed similar qualifications, which is what led me to believe that they were fundamentally the same. They were educated in the fields of psychiatry and primary care to provide necessary interventions for the improvement of health. I grew to understand that varying values and belief systems existed among the staff, and these were shaped by their experiences in life, including religious and cultural aspects.

I began recognizing these differences as various staff approached me in my office to discuss their concerns. For some, the most concern was making sure the work was evenly allocated at all times. Other staff members were more concerned about ensuring the possibility of overtime for the future. Still others came to me wanting another professional's work quality to improve. And finally, others wanted to assure me they were doing the best they could.

It became clear that I had to maintain an open-door policy. This reassured staff that I would listen to their concerns and take action when necessary. I would follow up on discussions via face-to-face interactions or email. If there was a conflict among staff, I addressed it immediately.

The tools I used during my tenure included an open-door policy, transparency of work performed during my administration, and conflict resolution, including a formal meeting with involved parties to address the issue(s). When I decided to use these tools, my goal was not to promote cultural competency. Instead, it was to mirror a sense of fairness throughout the medical staff, promoting a sense of oneness among a diverse group of people.

Doctor A (Chinese female) constantly came to my office expressing concerns about the medical care of patients. She expressed genuine interest and fear that patients were not receiving the best possible care. After several visits such as this, I finally recognized the common thread of these scenarios. The covering physician, Doctor B (Filipino female), was involved in all of these cases due to cross vacation and days off. I began to review charts and realized that the medications prescribed for some of these patients were changed. This necessitated an intervention between the two physicians to understand and identify the effects of patient care.

After discussing my concern with other physicians, as well as reading information on the various cultures that I had begun to supervise, I noted different stereotypes that were documented about the Chinese and Filipino cultures regarding work ethic. The workers within the Chinese culture are stereotyped as hard workers, even to the point of exhaustion; whereas, the workers in the Filipino culture have been represented as slackers, and if possible, they would "mooch" off the work of others. After meeting with the Chinese physician and Filipino physician together, it was clear that one was very protective of her work and resented the other for the coverage she provided, viewed as inadequate. This process opened communication between the two of them in order to help both verbalize their concerns for patient care and their outcomes. I began to realize that an administrator's agenda for the department may be jeopardized due to the internal thoughts and ideas staff members brings with them to the job.

I wanted both Dr. A and Dr. B to attend a conflict resolution meeting. Arranging the meeting took some time, due to the doctors' apprehensions about meeting. The meeting was finally arranged, and I asked another administrator familiar with the situation to assist with the dynamics from an observation standpoint. During the meeting it became clear to me neither listened to the other, and each thought how they did things was the best and only way.

Doctor A was hesitant to address the concerns in front of Doctor B. I assisted by discussing Dr. A's concerns in a general way, and then I encouraged Doctor A to follow up with any additional details. She reluctantly discussed wanting patients to be cared for in an appropriate manner to the best of her ability. She remained resistant to discuss her primary issue which was related to the below average care that she perceived Doctor B was providing to the patient. Of course, Doctor B talked about her goal to provide the best care possible in a setting, with limited services.

It remained very difficult to address the element of suboptimal care that was perceived by Doctor A. I addressed my concerns as medical director, which consisted of patients receiving multiple changes in care during their stay and inconsistencies in information given to patients regarding the care provided.

The focus of the discussion centered around each person wanting to provide services that were adequate and most helpful to the patient. I encouraged each practitioner to remember that in medicine different providers can approach treatment in many different ways, but each with good outcomes.

The conversation did not move toward discussing anyone's inadequacies but embracing different treatment options and respecting that everyone does not approach treatment in the same manner. Reaching this goal did not occur immediately. Instead, we met several times to discuss patients the two physicians shared. Through this process, the two physicians improved communication to the point where their meetings could occur without my presence.

It was important for me to meet with the observer in between meetings in order to discuss the dynamics of the interactions between the two physicians. The observer noted that the non-verbal communication between the two physicians during the initial meetings indicated that the two physicians disliked each other. However, over the course of the three meetings the communication improved and facial expressions and body language improved.

It was never my intention that a full confrontation occur between the physicians. My plan was to hear each person's concerns, and to address them in a respectful way, and to understand that although we are all different, we are also alike in many ways.

In another situation, I was leading a medical staff meeting and one of the physicians stated, "You favor Doctor G because she is black." Initially, I was taken aback by the accusation. I was standing there, facilitating a staff meeting, and thinking that I was a pretty good medical director. The words surprised me. How does one respond to such a statement? How do you remain composed? I responded that it would be inappropriate to address the issue in the current setting. Nevertheless, Doctor C continued to say that I favored Doctor G, allowing Doctor G to take days off and denying days off for her. At that point, I began to talk about my emphasis on fairness, equality, and respect in the workplace. I could tell that everyone in the meeting was becoming extremely uncomfortable. So, I asked Doctor C if we could discuss the matter in a more private setting. She did not reply. Instead, she abruptly left the meeting.

How does cultural competency factor into this scenario? How does one lead a group of diverse staff in the midst of differences?

After the awkward exchange, I contacted Doctor C and asked her to come to my office so that her issues might be discussed. She arrived displaying a defensive posture, as if waiting for an angry state-ment from me. I quickly restated what she said in the meeting, and I apologized for making her feel that there was favoritism. I reiterated my stance on fair treatment for everyone.

Doctor C did not know that throughout my years in high school, college, and medical school, I also felt someone was being favored over me, or that someone was receiving the benefit of the doubt and I was not, and that someone was always receiving a pass when a mistake was made. She did not realize that my upbringing, my religious beliefs, and my culture had built inside me a sense of fairness. I did not want anyone to feel what I felt in the past.

I never want the people I lead to feel inadequate, self-conscious, unsure, and insecure. So, for her to say that about me was hurtful; it made me sad, and it made me take a closer look at myself. I asked myself the hard questions: Are you showing favoritism? Are you being fair to all? Are you helping others to feel insecure, as if they have no voice?

During our meeting, I welcomed her speculation. I encouraged her to share examples of instances where she perceived me to demonstrate favoritism. I wanted to know how I displayed this behavior. She slowly went through several scenarios: "You did not approve my vacation, you docked me for being late, you moved me out of an office and gave it to Doctor C."

As a I sat there, I began to think about my inadequate training in cultural competency, which consisted of a yearly computer module. How much did I really reflect on this material? How did it guide me in my day-to-day interactions with such a diverse staff? I realized that I never really thought about it until I had to repeat the module yearly. The cultural competency modules only addressed staff-to-patient interactions. There was no guidance regarding staff-to-staff communications and sensitivity.

I took the time to address the issues and attempted to help Doctor C understand that her time was denied due to others taking off; her time was docked due to the policy of the organization, and the office was addressed due to the fact that someone else had already claimed the office. Doctor C was unaware that the administration had approved the office assignment. I explained to her that many decisions occur without the staff's knowledge to avoid interruptions in day-to-day operations.

In retrospect, I recognize that even though policies in the organization did not change; I worked to lead in a culturally competent manner—of course, at the time, I did not have a name for my leadership style. Nevertheless, my goal was to provide transparency, help people feel part of the community and process, give staff members hope that change could occur, and provide an atmosphere of trust.

Victor T. Tan, Psy.D.

Clinical Psychologist

When One's Culture Conflicts with Intergenerational Values

When working with a population that was born in one country and migrated to the US, who have children born in the United States or are naturalized citizens, care should be taken in understanding the different levels of acculturation. In my experience in working with these families, the disconnect between the children and parents with regard to their attitudes, values, and experience can make it extremely difficult for them to appreciate each other's points of view, and this will impede their capacity to function cohesively as a family. The following examples are a culmination and blend of cases dealing with families with intergenerational and cultural discord.

The first, involves a Hispanic family of Mexican origin. Some Latin American households maintain the traditional cultural view of males being strong, protective providers, and females being self-sacrificing caregivers.

The mother in this study brought her teenage daughter to therapy complaining that the daughter wanted to go out, play sports, and socialize instead of staying home to care for her younger siblings, and helping with household chores and preparing meals.

The daughter didn't understand why her older and younger brothers had more freedom and liberties and almost no responsibilities compared to her. She complained to her mother that her friends in school had parents who treated their sons and daughters equally. "I want to spend time with my friends and in sports and activities I enjoy," she pleaded with her parents.

They were unsympathetic, and her defiance and acting out behaviors escalated. She started to ignore the after-school curfew, and began to procrastinate on her responsibilities at home, and the squabbles with her siblings intensified.

Her brothers joined her parents in chastising her, and they reminded her to be obedient. Her parents, desperate to maintain their authority, decided to ground her. She began to ignore her schoolwork and increased her interest in school friendships. The more her attention strayed from her studies, the more concerned her parents became as her grades declined. Her restrictions intensified and the conflicts in the home became more frequent. She became angry and resentful and eventually depressed and disheartened.

Her friends seemed to have the perfect life compared to hers. Their parents seemed caring and permissive compared to her cruel and mean parents. She began to withdraw from her family. She started to cut herself and harbor thoughts of death. She felt her environment closing in on her, and she wanted to escape her misery.

This mother and daughter were in a conflict over their different cultural upbringings. The mother was from a culture that taught her to be submissive, self-sacrificing and subservient, while the daughter had been exposed to the more prominent middle-class American culture that celebrates individualism.

Dana (1993) wrote that the Anglo-American World View and Practice may be characterized as individualism: consisting of independence, autonomy, locus of control, self-interest, and self-actualization. Competition is promoted. Power and status are defined by money, titles and possessions. English is the spoken language, eye contact, physical boundaries, controlled emotions are the communication standard, and are just some of what defines the dominant Anglo-American worldview.

In contrast, the Hispanic culture is primarily a patriarchal structure that attributes authority to the father or oldest male relative. The male is respected for their machismo: physical strength, aggression and sexuality. The female is prescribed the role of Marianismo: submissive, obedient, dependent, gentle, and nurturing. Women are expected to devote themselves to cooking, cleaning, and caring for their children and husbands. The family unity is paramount, and the expectation is "the father is the head of the family, the wife takes care of the children, and children must behave according to the father's rules" (Paniagua, 1994).

Per CDC's Healthy Communities program, *Building Our Understanding: Culture Insights Communicating with Hispanic/Latinos*, "The traditional patriarchal structure grants the father or oldest male relative the greatest power, whereas women are expected to show submission" (Kemp & Rasbridge, 2004). In addition, "Hispanics come from a collectivistic culture where group activities are dominant, responsibility is shared, and accountability is collective. Because of the emphasis on collectivity, harmony and cooperation among the group tends to be emphasized more than individual function and responsibility" (Gudykunst, 1998).

The above case exemplifies the Intergenerational Cultural Dissonance common amongst families that are struggling to resolve their ethnic cultural upbringing, history, and values with the existing dominant cultural experience. The degree that children and adolescents and parents subscribe to, or are acculturated to, the prevailing dominant cultural views can greatly impact the parent-child relationship and subsequent responses.

Studies in the area of Intergenerational Cultural Dissonance (ICD), the "clash between parents and children over cultural values," focusing on immigration populations with minority populations—such as Asian, Hispanic, and African American populations—suggest that this "clash" is commonplace and can be considered the norm (Choi et al 2008).

In 2008, Choi, He, and Harachi did a study amongst Vietnamese and Cambodian immigrant families, and they found support for their contention that ICD increases parent-child conflict, weakening the parent-child bond, and increases the likelihood of behavior problems. They found much support in the literature that parent-child discord, as characterized by frequent disagreements, arguments, and expressed anger, make the child more susceptible to both externalizing problems, such as antisocial behavior, aggression, and substance use, and internalizing problems, such as depression and anxiety. However, they also observed much support for a close positive parent-child bond mediating and protecting against these adolescent problems, enhancing healthy social and psychological adaptation and coping.

Similarly, Wang & Benner (2016) found family cultural socialization important in how families shape the child's cultural heritage (racial or ethnic identity) and values, and this was associated with better socio-emotional and academic health (pp 12 -13).

As Camino observed, a therapist working with a patient from a different culture should:

1. Address the cultural differences between the client and the therapist.

2. Assess and treat the client as an individual, less as therapists we wrongly attribute stereotypes to the client and family or miss cultural characteristics that are present.

3. That therapist should examine their own values, beliefs and attitudes so one doesn't erroneously prescribe these onto them clients.

4. Educating clients by explaining the nature and process of a clinical assessment and the questions asked about family, psychiatric, developmental and trauma history can alleviate and clarify the client's misperceptions, anxieties, distrust or skepticism about the therapist's orientation, goals and approaches, in order to align with the client (Camino et., al, 1999, p. 130).

After developing an appreciation of how the family subscribes to the above issues, the therapist helps the family listen to each other and their values and needs. This can best be done by identifying an area of conflict and assisting the family in sharing their perspectives and experiences based on their cultural upbringing and degree of acculturation to the dominant or mainstream culture.

In my case example, the parents came here from Mexico and the children were born here. The parents are fluent enough conversation-ally to not require translation, and the teen helps when needed. All the children are educated in English, and they can understand some Spanish but do not speak it at home or with their peers.

The mother was encouraged to share about her life growing up in Mexico and her female role, and why she believes her daughter's womanly role is the same. The daughter was encouraged to explain how she sees the female role currently and why her values are different than her parents. They (mother and daughter) then addressed common values, such as respect and helping with household responsibilities. The mother agreed that her daughter should have some liberties, if they did not interfere with her studies and helping her with the house.

The American culture is not one single entity, but the unique combination of many cultures of many people; some people are native and others have migrated over the centuries to North American. The country can be extremely diversified depending on the state, city, county or even the residential street one lives on. Diversity is observed in people's activities, values, and customs one participates in and surround themselves with (Shearer 2008). Thus, the reference to the American culture as a salad or mosaic, giving appreciation to the idea of multiculturalism, instead of the metaphor of a melting pot, which symbolized assimilation, is more appropriate.

So, how does intergenerational cultural dissonance cross paths with intergenerational discord? What does it mean to be culturally sensitive to intergenerational conflict?

Intergenerational discord or dissonance may be defined in a number of ways. For purposes of the essay, the focus is not on generations defined by a particular set of birth years, such as between Generation X vs Millennials, but centers on the conflicts between the younger versus the older generation and more specifically the struggles between adolescents and adults.

Being culturally sensitive to intergenerational conflict isn't just about identifying a family's particular ethnic or racial identity: i.e., Caucasian, African American, Native American, Hispanic or Asian. It is not about having a broad appreciation of their general values, customs and family hierarchy. It is much more specific. It is about understanding the individuals that make up a particular family and their life experiences.

Just as within an ethnic or racial population, a family may belong to much smaller subcultures, with different languages, customs, and values, i.e., the many different tribes that make up the Native American populations, and similarly in Chinese society, the different dialects spoken in different regions, provinces and prefectures.

Ideally the task of a capable therapist has to be the non-judgmental willingness to listen for how the different generations within a family view their world and each other. The therapist helps the generations listen to each other's worldviews, values and expectations so in their understanding of the other they are better equipped to communicate and negotiate in order to meet each other's needs.

As therapists, working with children, teens and their families, we are not just about establishing obedience and respect. Often the issues are related to emotional distress and acting out behaviors associated with differing interests, motivations, values and viewpoints.

It may seem intuitive or even obvious that the closer the members of the family are in relation to their level of acculturation to the predominant population, or the smaller the difference in age between parents and their offspring, that they would be more understanding and appreciative of each other's perspectives, thereby reducing the level of conflict between them. However, this isn't a given.

As therapists and clinicians, we should remind ourselves that we work with a skewed population, who seek assistance because they are experiencing great struggles with family dysfunction. Unlike more healthy families that have learned to manage and work through their conflicts without needing professional intervention, our families find themselves in dissonance.

This is not to diminish the value of lessons learned about the major culturally diverse groups, as they serve to help inform the culturally competent therapist with population-specific information that guide our assessment and interventions. Rather, paying attention to the details of our family's history and experiences prevents the therapist from accidentally misconstruing or underappreciating the clients and their families we serve, and their different ideas and values, and thereby avoid assuming that their worldviews are similar to ours.

My focus in addressing this topic is not to address any specific cultural dissonance amongst the different racial or ethnic majority or minority population. Instead, my attempt is to shed light on how family members' unique heritage, level of acculturation, values and needs, impact on how parents and children interact, and contribute to parent-child conflicts and susceptibility to behavior and acting out problems in their lives.

In a parallel tract, intergenerational dissonance is the conflict between the parent's desire for unity and the children striving for autonomy. The child's need to separate oneself from the family is a natural developmental course in establishing one's identity and independence. In contrast, the parent's focus on the family unit tends to counter this developmental journey, setting the stage for potential conflict with the adolescents striving for autonomy and their own individualism.

Over my years of clinical practice working with children, adolescents and parents, a frequent theme of contention between the generations, youth and adult, is "to understand and be understood."

Adolescence itself is a challenge to the family hierarchy and unity as it is a natural developmental process, a rite of passage towards independence. The adolescent's journey towards adulthood is a perilous one, and tends to contest existing family roles, as the youth experiment with his or her own ideals, values and affiliations.

Teens these days are surrounded by technology, and obsess about electronics, cellphones, video games, web surfing and online social networking. They are preoccupied with friendships, peer acceptance and affiliation. They struggle with their identity, sexuality, academics, sports, material possessions, clothing, appearance and drugs. At the same time, they have to balance their roles with their family and their desire for independence and autonomy.

References

Canino, I. A. & Spurlock, J. (1994) *Culturally Diverse Children and Adolescents: Assessment, Diagnosis, and Treatment.* New York, The Guilford Press.

Choi, Y., He, M. & Harachi, T.W. (2008). Intergenerational Cultural Dissonance,

Parent-Child Conflict and Bonding, and Youth Problem Behaviors among Vietnamese and Cambodian Immigrant Families. *Journal of Youth Adolescence, 37* (1): 85-96.

Dana R. H. (1993) *Multicultural Assessment Perspectives for Professional Psychology.* Boston, A Longwood Professional Book.

Gudykunst, W. B. (1998). *Bridging differences: Effective intergroup communication.* Newbury Park, CA: Sage.

Jenkins A. H. (1995) *Psychology and African Americans: A humanistic Approach.* Boston, A Longwood Professional Book.

Kemp C, Rasbridge L. (2004) *Refugee and Immigrant Health: A Handbook for Health Professionals:* New York: Cambridge University Press.

Lee C. C. (1995) Ed. *Counseling for Diversity: A Guide for School Counselors and Related Professionals.* Boston, A Longwood Professional Book.

Paniagua F. A. (1994) *Assessing and Treating Culturally Diverse Clients: A Practical Guide.* Thousand Oaks, CA. Sage Publications

Shearer, Benjamin F. Series (2008) *Culture and Customs of North America.* Westport, Connecticut Greenwood. eBook., Database: eBook Collection

Stevick R. A. (2014) *Growing Up Amish: The Rumspringa.* John Hopkins University Press.

Wang, Y. & Benner, A.D. (2016) Cultural Socialization Across Contexts: Family-Peer Congruence and Adolescent Well-Being. *Journal of Youth and Adolescence.* 45 (3) p. 594, 18 p.

Diane Washington, M.D.
Adult and Geriatric Psychiatrist

"Baby, my kitty-kat been bothering me!"

Oh, the days of Meyer House at Michael Reese Hospital. It was 1988 when I became intimately aware of what "health disparities" truly meant.

Meyer House in 1988 served as the inpatient hospital units for the indigent patients with public aid and/or without any form of healthcare insurance. It was uniquely set apart from the main hospital through a series of intricate underground tunnels and or winding corridors dependent on the route taken.

Wow! Being the on-call intern for Meyer House was an eye-opening experience, and I knew from the beginning that this experience would somehow directly mold, shape, and build my subsequent healthcare career path.

Patient room 212: Picadilly, C.

I entered into the patient's room to perform a history and physical exam. I introduced myself,

"Hi, Ms. Picadilly, my name is Dr. Washington, and I need to ask your permission to perform a physical exam and to get some medical information."

"Get my permission?" Ms. Picadilly replied.

I was saddened by what I saw and experienced while on the rotating call schedule of 1:3 (every third night on-call duty). These were "my people" suffering from chronic diseases and obviously segregated from the main house hospital based on ability to pay. I remember so vividly the ominous question asked by the unit clerks, "Do you have private insurance? Do you have public aid or no insurance?" Like robots, they spat out these questions without any empathy for a patient's dire conditions.

My time at the Meyer House served as an awakening for me. Even today, as I think of those experiences, they seem surreal. It was almost like the events were dreams, but they were reality.

Meyer House treated the most chronic medical conditions ever seen due to a multitude of contributory factors: lack of access to care, inability to pay, simple neglect, denial of health conditions, and ultimately, inability to afford the cost of medications. Not to mention the chronic recidivism of being in and out of the hospital with a multitude of transient healthcare providers, making it cumbersome to get through the process and achieve some health stability. So, I humbly submit this case scenario as an illustration of cultural competence.

I was the intern on call and received an admission to Meyer House from the emergency room. This was an eighty-three-year-old black female who was having multiple medical issues. I entered into the patient's room. I had been up for twenty-four hours due to an exhausting night of on-call responsibilities primarily the inpatients on the Meyer House units. As an intern, I covered most of the hospital when on call. However, it was always known by the medical house staff that "you could get stuck on Meyer House and would be there all night," despite the additional units needing medical coverage.

The patients on Meyer House were the sickest, most chronic, and most difficult patients to manage. They required and needed your undivided attention, as well as a little patience and respect.

"Good morning Ms. Picadilly, *yes*, I must have your permission to take a medical history and perform a physical examination on you."

"Baby, that's the first time anyone in this hospital has asked my permission to do anything."

Startled by the disclaimer, it brought me back to my medical school days at Southern Illinois University in Springfield. The medical school days warrant another chapter, but I will say one positive thing about this institution: they taught me my bedside manner. I learned how to talk with patients to gain the most optimal amount of medical information to help guide treatment decisions. To this day, I can say this small piece of the educational curriculum has served me quite well as a healthcare provider.

I digress, let's get back to the case. Trying not to get into to a lengthy discussion about Ms. Picadilly's response, I nodded my head, and with direct eye contact assured her that I clearly understood her statement. She then agreed to the task at hand of performing the History & Physical Exam (H&P).

While initiating the medical history, Ms. Picadilly looks up at me and says, "You's a pretty black gal, and you a doctor, too! I am so proud of you baby, but can you help me out? The first thing you can do for me is give me something for this binding."

"Binding? What's that?"

"I can't go. I'm all locked up and ain't gone in weeks. Can you give me something to make me go?"

"Okay, I will make sure we get something to take of care that problem, but let's finish with the medical history so I make sure we cover everything."

We proceeded with the medical history.

"Are there any other problems that you have been experiencing over the last few months?"

"Baby, my kitty-kat has been bothering me, and it has been that way for a very long time now. I've been in and out of the hospital many times, and I always tell the doctors, but they don't pay me no attention.

The last time that 'white' doctor came in and I told him about it, he went to looking under the bed as if he was going to find a cat. I asked him what he was looking for, and he replied, 'There are no cats allowed in the hospital.'"

Okay, so the SIU medical training did not work here. I knew I was supposed to have a poker face and not respond emotionally to patient issues, but this time I could not contain my laughter. We both laughed aloud.

I used this opportunity as the "icebreaker" to facilitate a good, comprehensive conversation about an extremely difficult subject to broach with a woman her age. We were able to talk candidly about her real concerns regarding a subject that she previously found extremely difficult to articulate.

Ms. Picadilly stated she often would feel embarrassed about discussing this so, "I just let it go." She stated that she was glad I was a woman and felt that "it was a godsend when you walked through that door."

We talked about her "kitty-kat." I explained to the patient that the appropriate name was vagina, which she should say instead of "kitty-kat" when communicating with doctors. I asked her to repeat it and to refer to it by that name when discussing it medically. She agreed and thanked me.

The term "kitty-kat" was familiar to me; it was used by her mother and grandmother. In African American families, it was once taboo to speak openly about anything related to the female organs. Kitty-kat became a "code word" during discussions amongst Southern black women as a means to keep men from understanding what the women were talking about. Many men from many cultural perspectives around the world view problems related to the female organs system as an attestation of a women's limitations to fertility and/or sexuality.

Sometimes we need to go back in time and think about the era and experiences in which our patients have encountered or experienced. Understanding this perspective can be reflective of their medical presentations and descriptions of their physical ailments and/or psychological scars.

I believe I liberated Ms. Picadilly that day. The eighty-three-year-old female could not speak freely about a very personal feminine issue based on the era in which she grew up. As a result, she had an awkward way of relating and communicating the medical problem. It is understandable that she would have difficulty communicating this problem with a young, white, male doctor or any male for that matter.

In summary, Ms. Picadilly was an eighty-three-year-old female, widowed, lived alone, with no children. She had a history of obesity, diabetes with several bouts of DKA (Diabetic Ketoacidosis), a history of gastroparesis, hypertension, arthritis, and something with her "kitty-kat" was going on. Objective findings: a finger prick (quick test for blood sugar level) is over 350; BP (blood pressure) 169/125, abdominal distention with tenderness and hard mass in the lower abdomen. She was most likely obstructed from lack of bowel movements in several weeks; skin turgor was slow to recoil, nasal mucosal and mouth were dry (signs of dehydration). Bedsores were present on both buttocks (possible due to immobilization or bedridden state). Overall condition: was in a deteriorated state with denial of her current medical conditions.

She was a proud woman, who was trying desparately to hang on to her independence and way of life.

Beatrice Nelson Brewer, MD

Addiction Psychiatrist

Medical Director of Geriatric Psychiatry,

Methodist Hospital, Gary, In.

Personal Bias

Mr. S had been in treatment for opiate dependence for six months. He was being medicated with buprenorphine naloxone and was tolerating his treatment well. Since the initial admission evaluation, I had minimal interaction with him on weeks when he would pick up the prescription for his medication, which was fine with me.

He was a tall Caucasian male in his early thirties who presented with numerous tattoos on his arms and had a shaved head. While he was never anything but polite everything about his appearance screamed "Danger!" to me. My imagination fueled by my anxiety began to run a little wild. Was he a skinhead, a Nazi, or KKK member? I was in no hurry to find out.

During one of his visits, my nurse manager came into my office to inform me that his drug screen was positive for opiates and benzodiazepines. This meant that it was time to read him the riot act about using other substances with buprenorphine naloxone. His prescription pickup would now be weekly instead of monthly along with a drug screen to be sure that he was positive for buprenorphine and nothing else. How would he take this coming from me, an African American female psychiatrist? Would the plan be met with anger and arrogance? If I was to believe his appearance, he was used to being in control. Had he even done the first step of a twelve-step program? Was he ready to admit powerlessness over his addiction? How would I approach him?

It occurred to me that somewhere there was a common ground of what he would expect from someone providing medical care for him.

I started with, "We got your urine drug screen, and we are worried about you. People are dying from opiates out there, and we don't want you to die."

He answered by telling me that "people mix things together." Things being drugs.

We talked about the high probability of dying from mixing "things." He told me he had already lost several friends to opiates. Tears filled his eyes as we talked about why he was still here on Earth. We spoke of his youth and that his possibilities were all still before him. He had a criminal record, but I assured him there was still time to get his life on the right track. I asked did he want a home, a yard, a dog, and a family? He didn't answer with words, but with tears in his eyes. We had connected on a level deeper than appearances and assumptions could take us.

And so, I learned that being a culturally competent physician means never forgetting… that more connects us than divides us. Accepting and appreciating differences as well as challenging our own assumptions is necessary if we are going to successfully make a positive difference in the lives of others.[26]

---

26   T'Challa (Black Panther) in Black Panther, Marvel Studios

Elisa P. Bell, M.D.

Dr. Elisa Bell

Child Adolescent and Adult Physiatrist

Cultural Competency

One never forgets the face and stare of a patient with schizophrenia. I first saw it early in my training on an inpatient adult psychiatry unit. Schizophrenia is unique in its character: the faraway look, an empty look with no affect, a cold stare. My patient SP was brought to the unit by the police department. She was homeless for three months after arriving in America from Bolivia, South America. She was odd but distant, no cold stare, and she would mumble to herself. With her restricted affect, she would answer questions as best she could in broken English. She did not have the stare but was odd and distant.

The police report said they were called to a shelter for a disturbance. When the police arrived, SP was in the corner of the main sleeping area talking to herself. The staff reported that SP argued with other occupants at the shelter. The staff confronted her, and she shouted at them and retreated to a corner still talking to herself and shaking.

When we met, I approached her quietly, and she responded calmly in broken English. She was poorly dressed for winter in thin clothing. I spoke to her every day at the inpatient psych unit, and she answered questions appropriately in her broken English. She slept well, with no disruptive behavior, and a good appetite. She was cordial and the staff considered her a loner. She interacted only when asked to join group sessions but did not talk freely or volunteer comments in group. The staff also noted she would kneel down with praying hands. Once on her knees, she looked up and spoke to the sky. She exhibited a normal mood with no tangential or manic symptoms. She never expressed suicidal/homicidal ideations or plans. She appeared to have average intelligence, and she hesitated to speak of her home life in Bolivia. My attending professor directed I prescribe Prolixin for SP, a medication often used with a diagnosis of paranoid schizophrenia.

After several months, nothing had changed: she continued to have a normal mood, no suicidal/homicidal ideations or plans, with no tangential, mania, paranoia, or agitation symptoms. She spoke only in broken English when approached one-on-one in a calm manner, and she continued to kneel and pray to the sky. Despite increases in Prolixin, her behavior was exactly the same as it was upon her arrival on the inpatient unit.

I decided to become curious about Bolivian culture, learning there are over thirty native ethnic groups in Bolivia, who practice different religions. One of the oldest indigenous groups, the Aymara people of Bolivia, practice the "Fiesta de las Natitas" (Day of the Dead). They recover their loved one's skulls and pray to their spirits. They adorn their skulls with hats and glasses and have them on exhibit. This event occurs every year on November eighth. In La Paz, there is a witches' market, selling voodoo trinkets and animal parts used in prayer rituals. While I often questioned my patient's diagnosis; I did not speak her language, and I did not understand her spiritual beliefs or rituals. I often wondered if perhaps she came to this country and had fallen on hard times and was placed in a shelter that was not welcoming to her language or her spiritual practices. Over the years, I have traveled to other Latin countries and witnessed them praying in a similar manner as my patient. Without strong language skills, both in English and Spanish, I did not penetrate what this might mean.

Years later, with new information and knowledge enhancing my own cultural competency, I see and recognize my cultural competency errors:

We need to understand her language and what she was trying to communicate. Our interpretation should not have been as broken as her spoken words. As professionals, we should have brought in an interpreter before diagnosis.

We need to have some understanding of her religious beliefs, since she came to the unit with the behavior already identified as a problem. We should not have accepted the shelter's classification of her behavior as our own. Not understanding if she was praying or responding to auditory hallucinations was a cultural error, and a medical misstep.

We never focused on her culture; we kept American/Western culture in the center focus and compared her to it. We had no knowledge of her cultural norms, and expected her to be like us. We compared her behavior to American behavior, not Bolivian. We diagnosed her mental health based on what might have only been cultural differences.

A culturally competent medical provider might have greatly reduced the chances of these three cultural competency errors occurring. All the examples from my colleagues and friends speak to the imperative for Cultural Competency training across America. If the five steps would have been followed in the SP case, I believe outcomes would have been more aligned culturally, leading to a more beneficial patient experience.

Let's review the five steps to begin the process of cultural competency:

1. Awareness - to acknowledge cultural differences and their importance; how does the patient's culture influence them to reach their goals and fulfill their needs?

2. Critical self-awareness - A. self-reflection B. patient's identity may have dimensions (intersectionality)

3. Knowledge - to know the character and complexity of a patient's culture

4. Skills - to communicate clearly and effectively: practitioner to patient, patient to practitioner

5. Empathetic understanding – to avoid stereotypes by acknowledging the patient's important cultural aspects[27]

---

27   Bassey and Melluish, "Cultural competency for mental health practitioners: A selective narrative review," *Counseling Psychology Quarterly, 26*, (2003):151-173.

Chapter Five:

Interviews.

Interview one:

Dr. Elisa Bell interviewed Tawara D. Goode and Suzanne Bronheim in Washington, D.C. at Georgetown University National Center for Cultural Competence.

Dr. Bell: Are there any quick guidebooks for learning cultural competency for clinical staff?

T. Goode: I generally say there is no quick way, and we should avoid the whole notion that cultural competence is just a workshop or one course or condensed to the content of a guidebook. So, if we look at the framework, at least that we use for cultural competency here at the National Center for Cultural Competence at Georgetown University (https://nccc.georgetown.edu), we look at cultural competence as first having congruent and defined values and principals. This would be within a system and/or an organization where those values and principals guide policy, structures, practices, behaviors and attitudes. This enables employees and the staff to work effectively cross culturally. That framework often develops over a period of time. We view cultural competence as a developmental process where different people, different organizations, and different systems occupy different places on a cultural competence continuum. In my view, even if there were quick guidebooks, I would not recommend them because CC is an ongoing intentional process both on the part of both organizations and individuals.

Dr. Bell: Have there been any new developments within the last few years in cultural competence training for medical practitioners at any level?

T. Goode: Cultural competence covers very broad areas and touches upon many different aspects in medical education. So, in the last five years, the medical profession has placed increased emphasis on thorough, implicit or unconscious biases in medical education. We have a really tremendous Continuing Medical Education (CME) program that we created for rheumatology to address conscious and unconscious biases.

Now, we will focus on lupus as an area where healthcare disparities disproportionally impact African Americans and other women of color[28]. The great majority of CME, available on the GTU website, helps us understand both conscious and unconscious biases and their impact on the overall health and well-being of diverse populations so we can address them in the context of medicine. So, that's one area, although not new, increasingly a focus area relating to medical education and practitioners.

I also believe we have promoted the capacity to engage in cultural competence self-assessment, as well as look at cultural and linguistic competence self-assessments. We have created one of the very few

---

28   Bell, Elisa. Lupus is 9 times more prevalent in women than men. 90% of Lupus patients are women. Lupus is 2-3 times more prevalent in Minority women i.e., African Americans, Hispanic/Latinas, Asian, Alaska Natives, Native Hawaiians, other Pacific Islanders than among Caucasian women .

validated measures of cultural competence and linguistic competence in collaboration with colleagues at Case Western Reserve University. The measure was published in 2014 in *Medical Care*, a fairly prestigious journal. Using this tool, we've been able to look at how to measure cultural and linguistic competence at the practitioner level. This is an emerging area needing a lot more emphasis and research.

We've created an instrument to measure cultural competence and linguistic competence in three areas:

First: what is it we as a practitioner know about culturally diverse communities and their health?

Second: If you know something, what do you do differently in your practice?

Third: If you know a little something, are you doing something different in your practice? What are you doing to support the health and well-being of communities that have often been disenfranchised?

So, we also have an interactive tool on our website that measures these three areas (https://nccc.georgetown.edu/assessments). We are very excited about the tool because it is interactive. We collect data on who is using it and how they respond to a series of questions. What the user gets is feedback on how they stand in the above three areas. In addition, users develop a plan outlining where they are and where they need to go in a world where cultural competence as something continuous and intentional. You also get a list of resources to help you on your journey, all available on our website. You should know we have validated and evaluated this tool thoroughly to measure cultural competence within a setting. The other critical area—and these are intersecting areas—is that cultural competence spans all of health-care literacy.

As we think about linguistic competence and how we define it, health literacy is a strong component. What we see increasingly in research literature, particularly the work of Rumer Rod and out of NIH, is that people understand the role of health literacy as much broader than what a patient may bring to any given encounter. We need to look at the role of healthcare organizations to ensure they have the capacity to meet health literacy needs of populations served. Since Healthy People 2010 and 20/20 Word Develop, there are different ways to address health literacy taking the onus from the patient, and placing it squarely in the lap of the healthcare community, hospitals, and others who serve and support patients.

Instructional competency basically says medicine is complex. We can't shift the burden of health literacy solely to the patient. Literacy demands the ability to negotiate systems, understand consent, navigate hospital systems, provide information about symptoms and another cluster of interests belonging to the patient, Literacy is a shared responsibility and does not leave healthcare practitioners off the hook. There are a number of tools practitioners use to help with health literacy issues, and more research is on the way. Research is also looking at the role of culture in health literacy so we do not separate cultural context from the people who seek our help. NIH has put together nice language around understanding culture. For me, cultural competence is simply understanding culture and integrating that into the work we do on behalf of communities.

Dr. Bell: I have to congratulate you on the measurements you've developed. Thank you for that. What percentage of American clinicians do you estimate are culturally competent?

T. Goode: I have no idea because that gets back to how you frame cultural competence. There are many levels of cultural competence and I would be very leery of anyone saying, "I'm culturally competent, I took this course" or "I'm culturally competent because I'm a person of color" or "I'm culturally competent for any variety of reasons."

Here, we look at cultural competence as an ongoing process. There are various levels of proficiency along this continuum and people bring their own experience to their work. I find it hard to say a person is culturally competent or not. For example, I may have traditionally worked in an all African American low-income community. Next I move to another community peopled by Latinos and very high-income African Americans. Does everything I knew and did in the first setting translate naturally to the new one? I don't think so!

For me, cultural competence remains an ongoing growth process shaped by what you know. But what I knew ten years ago is very different from what I know now. Consequently, labeling someone as "culturally competent" concerns me. While I do believe many behaviors and practices will come to describe levels of cultural competence, people can't rest there. CC study represents their ongoing commitment and their learning over time.

Dr. Bell: There's an ongoing debate centered on the premise that doctors of a certain race should treat patients of the same race because of possible better treatment outcomes. What new research discusses the benefits of having African American doctors treat African American patients?

T. Goode: There is some data to speak to this, but then there is also data that conflicts with that statement. After interviewing African American patients in several studies, they felt African American doctors understood them better, could relate to them, and didn't judge them. Yet, there are other studies looking at African American physicians who may not necessarily demonstrate the same behaviors. A lot of the differences have to do with culture. There are African American physicians who chose to commit to serving African American communities. But we cannot forget about culture and its socio-economic status and education. I don't accept that all African American physicians are better at treating African American patients because that negates the impact of cultural competence. When we look at cultural competence in this way, practitioners have to be competent for whoever walks in the door whether this person is African American, Latino, LGBTQ, or elderly. Who they are and where they come from matters. We always need to deal with culture as well as racial and ethnic differences.

We need more research; but a compelling body of studies address doctors who have gone to medically underserved areas, chose to stay work, are African American and part of the community. When I served in the National Service Corp back in the day, several African American physicians went to work in Latino or non-Hispanic white Appalachian communities. They succeeded as essential physicians, but also because they understood and overcame cultural resistance and became the physicians of choice in a diverse the population. This is cultural competence--not racial, not ethnic, but *cultural* competence. We are all cultural beings. Yet we have to look at race and ethnicity as aspects of culture, not the only aspects to consider.

Dr. Bell: You've answered a lot of questions, but I think I've got to ask a second part to this question. Is there research about why doctors who largely treat African American/minority patients have very good treatment outcomes after he or she has received cultural competence training?

T. Goode: The article we wrote when we validated the cultural competence practitioner assessment included data on when and if folks had training. We learned those who reported training in cultural and linguistic competence fared much better than those who did not. I don't know the extent the literature looked specifically at white doctors, African American ones, and/or other minority patients having better outcomes after they've received training. My colleague Dr. Joseph Betancourt has engaged in some work, as has Glenn Flores. I believe

Glenn is doing amazing and prolific work that as contributed significantly to the literature. In general, literature on cultural and linguistic competence has varied over the years, especially when more funding was available. Now research is dependent on individual interest.

Dr. Bell: Thank you. Is there a specific issue pertaining to cultural competency that should be addressed and/or needs priority?

T. Goode: How we understand cultural competence remains critical. If we frame cultural competence as only a "minority issue," this is a disservice because culture is not simply race or ethnicity. What needs to happen and what we need to talk about is intersectionality. Intersectionality is essential and critical. In my presentations I note how we focus on African American populations or Latino populations or other populations without addressing if I am female, gay, have a disability, or have kids. All of those characteristics intersect, so we have to consider multiple cultural identities, without so much focus solely on race and ignoring the myriad within-group differences among racial and ethnic groups. Intersectionality is key and critical.

We cannot ignore population health but we must also address poverty. For example, when a particular person sits in front of you, can you ascribe those things you know about population to this one person? I don't think so. We have this whole notion of intersectionality that we are all cultural beings and bring many different identities to the table. How do we address that in medicine and what is the role of cultural and linguistic competence? I would say that would be an area to explore further.

Dr. Bell: Since the implementation of your website, what percentage of clinicians have been through your cultural competence training?

T. Goode: I have data on folks who have gone through the cultural competence health practitioner assessment. Today, in terms of training, it has become very tailored and individualized. We no longer give general training. Instead we do numerous presentations across the country serving healthcare providers, practitioners, educators, administrators, etc. For each audience, we design the content based on "the who" we are speaking to and "the what" is the theme. We receive federal funding and for some groups, we collect data and information, and for other groups, we do not. For many years, we were funded by the Bureau of Permanent Healthcare, doing training for clinicians and in community health centers across the country. That funding is no longer available but we are currently still collecting data. You will see on our website significant accomplishments for health resources, service administrators and the federal government. I can share outcomes.

We've also looked at practitioners; however, you have to have a home for cultural competence practice. It doesn't really matter how culturally competent I am, if I'm in an organization that doesn't support policies, procedures, and resources for CC. I can only do so much. Our other message is that cultural competence is not just at an individual level. It must also reside at the organizational and system levels. Unless an organization addresses all levels, you are not promoting cultural competence. We capture every level: cost generation, administrator, practice and service delivery, patient and family, individual, and community. Our aims seek to impact all levels. However, the literature has largely zeroed in on the practitioner level--only one of many. The practitioner is then supported by policies, procedures, and resources.

Dr. Bell: Of those trained, what percentage have had a good treatment outcome? What percentage are minority status and what percentage are white status?

T. Goode: I absolutely do not know! We do not measure that. We also have a gap in our research. There are a number of studies showing the training that we do but there are also a number of research studies that have looked at cultural competence interventions and treatment.

We also did a paper in 2006, a commission from the Caldwell fund called *The Evidence based for Cultural Competence in Healthcare*. We looked at the literature at the time around advocacy of cultural and linguistic competence. It was a significant contribution to the field.

Dr. Bell: Have many organizations, institutions, federal/state/local governments, hospitals contacted you for training?

T. Goode: Hundreds, hundreds (laugh). That's how blessed I am!

Dr. Bell: Are you aware of a culturally competent medical healthcare facility that has experienced a decreased in healthcare disparities and improved in outcomes?

T. Goode: There are some examples documented in the literature. Is the entire facility having positive outcomes? Or are there only certain departments or programs? I want to make that point because there are documented interventions on culturally competent programs around diabetes. I'd be hard-pressed to say if they did that around diabetes, they are doing it across the board in the facility. I can identify programs that have culturally competent practices, but I would be uncomfortable endorsing an entire facility.

Dr. Bell: Do you think the federal/state/local governments will soon mandate cultural-competent training in our medical institutions, including medical schools, nursing schools, etc.?

T. Goode: I don't know about the federal/state/local governments, but I will share with you outcomes from a study we did for the Robert Wood Johnson Foundation. We looked at the policies in place at the federal level, specifically those mandating cultural-competence certification training. At that time, there were thirteen states with mandated training around cultural and linguistic competence; i.e., New Jersey, Washington State as the early adapters. We saw state level requirements but also the AAMC has requirements. We can point you to those in terms of what needs to be included in medical education--cultural competence is clearly there. However, it depends on the state and the state legislation. In our Robert Wood Johnson study, California had specific mandates for CME training. They looked at how CME integrated cultural and linguistic competence into their ongoing efforts with a requirement for three hours of training. New Jersey adopted a similar plan to a great degree of resistance as we learned from a colleague at Rutgers University who is very active in CC. We documented this into a study looking at cultural competence in the American health system. We also worked with two European journals to trace the history of cultural and linguistic competence from the legislative perspective. The federal government also mandates requirements through programs.

The National Class Standards we discussed are largely voluntary with the exception of standards impacting language access in Title Six. Title Six prohibits discrimination against anyone because of national origin--language is an aspect of national origin. You can't discriminate. Any entity receiving federal funds will provide language access services for individuals with limited English proficiency or who are monolingual. The law requires healthcare institutions to comply, period. How do you deal with this when there are federal statutes impacting at least some aspects of cultural competence relating to language? States have requirements for CME and AAMC also accredits schools of medicine identifying additional requirements. Local governments also add requirements, not necessarily for cultural competence training, but maybe for medical practice.

Dr. Bell: Based on what occurred with the current administration regarding Obamacare, will this increase socialized medical care to keep costs down (structural competency)?

T. Goode: This is a difficult question. It's not just the current socio-political climate in this country, it is part of a set of grounding principles in US society that we hold true: freedom. Whenever any group is "forced" to do something we give up freedom even if the concept may be helpful. Folks often rebel because they want freedom of choice regardless of the consequences for their neighbors or others in the community. The term "socialized medicine" frames the issue in a way that makes it hard to go there. We perceive socialized medicine and how politicians talked about it as a huge barrier—and that's simply socialized medicine--let alone the world of cultural competence and how it impacts how we deliver care. As a community we have not delivered the message to help people understand that cultural competence is not only for racial and ethnic groups other than non-Hispanic white because that is the definition of culture. Agreed that many groups: African American, American Indian, Alaskan Natives, Latino groups have more in the way of healthcare disparities--I'll come back to that. But there needs to be a focus. Unfortunately, in doing so, people confuse cultural competence as "oh, we don't have many people in our neighborhood or community who look like that, so it's not relevant." They fail to understand it's not racial/ethnic specific--it's about the capacity for addressing culture.

Dr. Bell: As a Child/Adolescent Psychiatrist, how can I effectively encourage the clinical community to acknowledge and possibly institute cultural competency in their training programs and practice?

T. Goode: For a group of scientists and practitioners, they want evidence. They are moved by evidence. How and when we produce evidence is very important. Most practitioners want the best for their patients and the communities they serve. Using these approaches will reduce barriers, improve access, improve utilization of care and consequently, improve outcomes. So, practitioners and researchers need to generate evidence and develop practices to help patients improve their care—a critical requirement. That said, we have to figure this out in a way that foregoes more schooling or adds unproven theories to their practices. We need to find ways for practitioners to merge their own cultural advocacy into what they do every day. CC is not something separate and apart, its integrated. People should be have recognized for the CC work they do whether in their practice or their associations. Let's find a strategic way to incorporate CC for the good of all.

Introductions: Tawara Goode introduces Dr. Bell to Suzanne Bronheim, who was present for Goode's interview.

Dr. Bronheim: I'm Suzanne Bronheim, and I've been at the center for forty-three years (this center, not the National Center). I am a clinical psychologist, and some of my work has been with children with special healthcare needs, people with disabilities, morphing into making things better and less fragmented for those folks.

Until I started work here, I wanted to be involved in all those areas, and continue to work with children with special healthcare needs. But my efforts evolved into strong interests in SIDS, safe sleep, infant mortality, cultural competence, and how these relate to infant mortality. Actually, there are as many stillbirth infant deaths as other causes, and the similarities are many. We have many families who lose their babies, but there is a much heavier burden in African American, American Indian, and Native Alaskan communities.

Rapes in these communities are three to four times greater than for white families. Also, many Hispanic families have better outcomes than white families. While smoking during pregnancy may be a factor, there is also evidence that the stresses of racism may also be in play. The literature notes how stresses of racism may impact infant mortality, particularly with pre-term and low birth weight, making these babies very vulnerable.

Actually, when you look at African American moms, and also across the whole socio-economic spectrum, people say, "Well, it's cause they're poor," right? However, well-educated, well-off African

American moms still see disparities compared to their counterparts in other races. Interestingly its worse than the disparity for poor folks because poor white folks don't do as well as rich white folks. Something different is happening and researchers should dive deeper into this issue.

They address the issue of how the health of the mother impacts the health of her baby. The facts suggest how the mom developed over time and the relative wealth of her father predicts outcomes for babies. For example, when families arrive from Africa, they don't have these disparity outcomes because the families are well off. Cultural competence has also had relevance. One is around the issue of bereavement support, and unfortunately, funding for bereavement support is much diminished.

We hope to add bereavement to the Head Start Health Group as a topic for physical and mental health this year. Bereavement and how you support people are tremendously culturally bound. The stigma for seeking mental health support in African American communities and some Native communities coupled with the fact that babies have died terrifies everyone.

We've discovered two relevant points. SIDS drove big parent movements to get government attention and get legislation passed. But many of the parent advocacy movements in America are organized by upper-middle-class white people who were shocked the system didn't work right for them when it always works right for them. So, they got angry and got something going. They started doing "Back to Sleep" campaigns and other initiatives. While SIDS rates dropped dramatically, disparities got bigger among races. While we now have a lot of bereavement folks, the parent support organizations are culturally, racially and completely different.

People used to ask, "How can we get people who lost children to come to our support group?" I said, "Do you want to talk about how you can make sure to get bereavement support? We can, but I don't think I can get them to your support group--not going to work!"

We did one project with First Candle, one of the bereavement organizations. A young African American woman who had done a lot of bereavement support said "I'm so sick of hearing families from my communities saying their church gave them no support. The best they would get is God needed another angel. You're only given what you can manage, and people are just not dealing with it."

So, we developed a set of curriculum modules. We were informed by a group of ministers and others in the faith community who put together a set of modules for clergy and church leaders to help them figure out how they can do a better job with bereavement. Culturally their faith is where families look for comfort, and they are not getting it. We learned some hair-raising stories. We often found that bereavement institutions in the African American communities felt lost or unable to support people in ways they needed. I wanted to take you through this because our website is dense, and we're ready to reconfigure African American faith-based bereavement modules. They are absolutely amazing.

Video testimonies and content are also plentiful in the modules. When you think about your role as a psychiatrist, when faith is not enough and folks need to differentiate between grief and when there are true psychological needs. Our work around cultural competence is broad and continues to be so.

How do you make a good referral? We also heard from families: "I'm just not getting over this" and then their religious institution would say to them, "You don't want to go see those people, keep it in the church, we are enough for you, or your faith isn't strong enough."

Elisa P. Bell, M.D.

We also heard from some pastors, "Yes, sometimes I sent my people for mental health support and the providers were inappropriate, culturally inappropriate. They don't take into account people's deep faith and how that works. They try to undermine us." This is a complex issue, but you have the responsibility to get to know people and find out who they are and make sure your people get it and to know how to present it, so it doesn't feel like rejection or a big stigma.

We also have video talking about the stigma in African American communities around depression and other mental issues. So, bereavement is one piece. The flip side covers health promotion, safe sleep, and back to sleep.

T. Goode: I commend Suzanne for this work. Suzanne led the work and pulled together this amazing product. Suzanne is a spiritual being, and in a strong faith, Jewish. I saw her transcend belief systems to find what she had in common with people. No matter if it was Christian versus Jewish, she took the perspective of both Christian and the African American communities to come up with these incredibly useful modules!

Another piece on our website covers the biopsychosocial model of care, looking at cultural competence within that lens. Here are some ideas we also created over time that don't fit neatly under the heading cultural competence training. Yet culture impacts so many things. When we face the future, here's what I see as the future of cultural competence. To me, we have to look at a vast number of nations, at mental health therapy, or at genetics and say okay, this is what you do. This is the role of cultural language. This is the lens we've brought and this is the reason we've been successful.

We've also done organizational assessments at the practitioner level for capacity. We've done organizational assessments of cultural competence and linguistic competence for large, public healthcare entities. We made an assessment for the Mississippi State Department of Public Health and an assessment for the state of Delaware. Folks use our tools and Suzanne gets lots of requests. Major hospital centers also want to use our tools, especially the Cultural and Linguistic Competence Policy Assessment. So, our work doesn't fit neatly into this tiny category.

Dr. Bronheim: What and for whom is cultural competence required? I get calls like, "Can you come out and certify us as culturally competent?" and I say, "Mmm, well????"

Dr. Bell: That was my next question: have other clinicians come forth for your help in this area?

Dr. Bronheim: People ask for help, but certifying as culturally competent? I wish I could say yes, as it would be a great fundraiser for the center. We're not talking about cultural competence in a global sense, one size fits all sense. Instead it's how does CC apply to what you do? Even when we consult with organizations on what cultural competence looks like for a person. We did a study on the front desk because so many families say, "The doctor wasn't bad, but my god, the way the people at the front treated me was horrible!"

T. Goode: Cultural competence starts at the front desk.

Dr. Bronheim   So, what does cultural competence mean for each person and their role? We talk a lot about clinicians. As mental health professionals, we spend time with people but primary care doctors get maybe 15 minutes. How do other folks think about it? I once had a woman call me and say, "We had this terrible incident and we picked up families and brought them to the hospital. The bus driver was horrible to the parents, racist. I don't know what was said. But I don't know what to do!" I said, "Well, you're a social worker and I'm sure your education included a lot about culture and cultural competence. So, I don't know if bus driver training goes over that. Did you go over

Elisa P. Bell, M.D.

this with them, give them any information or training? Why would you expect that?" What is a culturally competent bus driver? I'm not entirely sure. But, there's something there; but it's different from what the social worker did with the family when they got there. Cultural competence is not something abstract.

T. Goode: We get a lot of requests for assessments. We want to conduct Organizational Assessment Cultural Competence. It's like okay, we have experience and we have developed some tools. But why are you doing it--and there is silence. What is your goal? What do you want to do? If you want to do an assessment to look at what your clinicians know, that's different from how communities are engaged, or what are the policies and practices that are in place within your organization?

People think there is only one tool and you can use it to do a cultural competence organizational self-assessment. Our understanding of cultural competence has deepened over the years because we understand what culture is, including the culture of the organization. You can't separate all that when you look at what a clinician may do, what an administrator may do, what someone at the front desk may do, and what is the culture of the organization. As opposed to this huge focus on what are the cultural and racial compositions of the population the organization services.

Dr. Bronheim: Also, our professional culture. We all become acculturated into our profession. I remember when I was a psychology intern with a group of mental health professionals. I had trained the year before at Georgetown in the medical center where nobody was a mental health professional. You could see why they have a different cultural perspective on what patients are about. I'm sitting next in this meeting at the community health center and someone presents a case where they said, "Well, the child had five caregivers in the first two years. They're like, mmm..., they knew what that meant." I was like, "Really, you know what that meant? Can you explain it?" They explained and I went, "Oh, that's important." You continue to develop these belief systems and ideas of what your role is and what the patient's role is.

Suzanne shared an article about the many times that medicine doesn't think of itself as a culture. I loved that article because it said we're about science. So, it's not about a culture, it's about "we can prove this, this is what is going on." That's our viewpoint and I'm doing this in another study. I first get people to understand what culture is because in this country people always just equate culture to race and nothing else. So, getting people to have a much broader understanding is a prerequisite for cultural competence.

If you don't know what culture is, how are you going to talk about cultural competence? So, that's one issue. The other issue is around what people call it. I don't have to fight any more about "I don't want to call it cultural intelligence." I can't tell you all the different things people say. It's like, call it what you want to call it but this is what we're calling it, this is our framework for understanding it and we're comfortable with that. If some of our beliefs and practices fit your model, that's fine. I'm simply not entertaining the argument again about it should be cultural relevant, it should be cultural humility, and it's all of these things. Some, I feel were diversions from dealing what the true issues would be.

Dr. Bronheim: I've had the experience when we do this training because as the white person on the team, white people come up and say things to me (Ms. Goode, M.A.: That they won't say to me) and also, some will say, "I don't like the word competence. Are you saying I'm not competent?" I'll say, "I don't know you." But then they'll say, "If I'm not culturally competent, does that mean I'm a racist?" Again, I'll say, "I don't know you, but that's not what we're saying, but it's a piece of you to look at and think about," and then I give my little spiel about how we're all part of institutional racism. As white people, we benefit. We're saying we all have a culture.

Dr. Bell: This is a good point for me to close things out. First off, I would like to thank Suzanne for coming in on short notice and sharing her expertise. I want to congratulate her on her many years of service. She's very compassionate, very knowledgeable, and quite interesting. I wish I could pick your brain a little more, but thank you for sharing. Are there any last things as a Child/Adolescent/Adult Psychiatrist, and I started out as a pediatrician, is there any advice you can give me or last statements about how you feel about this interview? Have you learned anything from this interview? Is there anything you would like to share?

Dr. Bronheim: Having been a Child/Adolescent Psychiatrist, we don't take culture into account. We misread cues, we misread what we think are symptoms, or they may not even be symptoms, and we don't understand the pieces that can support change and growth in kids and families if we don't understand that content. It's just essential.

Dr. Bell: Thank you!

T. Goode: Spend time talking about what is culture and talking about that from multiple perspectives. If people basically don't understand their own culture, let alone the culture of the families and individuals they may be providing care, it makes things even more challenging. I can't tell you how many training sessions I've been to and I ask people to share one thing about their culture with the person next to them. People will make a face or say they can't share anything because they don't have a culture and it happens every time we do this work.

There's a lack of awareness about culture? How it manifests? How it influences our daily lives? And the fact that culture changes over time yet there are things that don't change.

This is an important component of cultural competence so that people don't narrowly think about cultural competence "the four-food-group approach." The stew of African Americans, the stew of Latinos, the stew of Asian Americans, and the stew of American Indians. So, it's like a formula and this is what you do with these four groups as opposed to understanding the huge array of cultural differences within those groups and addressing them in the provision of care.

Dr. Bell: Thank you!

Interview three:

Dr. Brian Griffin, MB, BCh, BAO

Director Cardiovascular Disease Training Program

The John and Rosemary Brown Endowed Chair in Cardiac Medicine, The Cleveland Clinic

Dr. Elisa Bell interviewed Dr. Brian Griffin

Dr. Bell: Thank you for being here today.

Dr. Griffin: It's a pleasure.

Dr. Bell: Cleveland Clinic has a commitment to diversity and providing staff with tools to improve cultural competency. How does Cleveland Clinic's commitment to cultural competency and diversity play out in terms of ongoing training for doctors and other staff members?

Dr. Griffin: I've been here for twenty-four years, and our commitment to diversity and recognition of different cultural backgrounds has really grown over time. A lot comes from the fact this a multicultural, diverse place. People come here from all over the world as physicians, nurses, other caregivers, and patients. We have people with incredible backgrounds. Like, it's not unusual on any given day to see someone from a Middle Eastern county in traditional garb and a few seats next to them, see somebody Amish, also in traditional garb. I can't think of too many places in the world where you see those sorts of traditions in the same place. I think this is what makes it such a unique and interesting place. Its proof of all the other things that come together here. We have lots of people from different parts of the world and we have major outreach.

This is a major referral hospital for all over the United States and the world, and yet, it serves an inner-city neighborhood in Cleveland with a population of relatively disadvantaged people. Our ability to encompass them has really improved over the last couple of decades, and we have become much more involved in the community around us than we were when I first arrived. Then we were on our own, and now we reach out to the community--and that's really good. We have a clinic in Fairfax, a Cleveland district that years ago nobody would talk about, but now we have embraced Fairfax. We are part of the Fairfax business district. We work with them to bring new businesses here.

We're also developing a new facility with IBM at the back of the hospital. IBM bought one of Cleveland's star companies, involved in computerized research. The new company will be headquartered here in what a was once a rundown copy area. Now it will be a new building very attractive for the community as a whole. The clinic has become much more mindful of the people around us, and seeks to have them get involved in their care and management.

Dr. Bell: Are the doctors trained? Do they get online training? If they do, how often?

Dr. Griffin: We have a really good system here, an online one called Comet. We learn about core competencies and take tests on the content. We study and test every number of years and diversity is one of the topics we also study. They're good because they're factual. We see things from other people's perspectives and it's so much easier to work with or relate to somebody when you can see through their eyes.

There are some things in each community that are different. For instance, I'm Irish, and the Irish are known for not liking people invading their personal space. They kind of have a shell around them and knowing when you deal with an Irish patient, you don't slap them on the back. You give them their space. The same is true with other communities, where we understand what is important to them and do a much better job.

For us too, we get people who don't know English or English is not their first language. This also requires effort to communicate because although we may have interpreters, the doctor-patient relationship requires a bond. Language is a great bond, but we have also been taught to work at other non-verbal cues to convey compassion or empathy to see where people are coming from.

I was head of our training program in cardiovascular medicine for eighteen years. It was the largest of its kind in the United States, and we had about forty fellows at the time. When I headed the program, we were a very diverse group. People from diverse cultural backgrounds make for an invigorated training program. So, the statue behind my desk is from the Association of Black Cardiologists of the United States awarded to our program for its success in promoting diversity. We're very proud of that.

Dr. Bell: There was an article in the Cardiology department at Northwestern by black men who said there needs to be cultural competency training at the medical school level.

Dr. Griffin: Clyde Yancy is head of Cardiology at Northwestern. As a physician or caregiver, you must immediately have empathy for people of diverse backgrounds and diverse lifestyles and its tricky. Physicians do not judge. Physicians and caregivers treat and provide care and support. It's hard to do when you don't look beyond your biases. You can train people, but if people don't work on it themselves then all the training in the world won't help them.

What resonates here is when people overstep or forget how they are indifferent or show attitudes that do not respect cultural and diverse backgrounds, we take them aside to challenge those attitudes. There is little or no support institutionally for these attitudes. We are tribal. People are tribal. Societies fashioned themselves as part of a tribe. You feel comfortable, safe, and secure in the tribe. When people are different from you, you often keep to yourself. It takes effort for people to explore outside of their natural instincts, inherited from our tribal makeup.

You have to look at yourself. We are made up of families. The smallest tribe is our immediate family then we go out from there. It requires an effort and some grace to look beyond that and to see everyone as part of our tribe.

Dr. Bell: How has a commitment to diversity impacted you personally?

Dr. Griffin: I've grown. I have a much better understanding of diversity now. I'm at a stage where I embrace and enjoy it--and my colleagues do, too. That's one reason we're here. Who doesn't what to have fun in a diverse place where you are challenged? If we are always in our own rough and bunker, we never grow. It's good to see what other people see.

What I enjoy about what I do here is that I see people from all over the world, every race, color, religion, etc. I see people who are extraordinarily wealthy and I see people who come from impoverished backgrounds. All of that is important. If all I saw were wealthy people, that isn't my mission. My mission isn't to treat well-off people.

What we do here is to provide high level care to people from different backgrounds. These people can't get it where they've been, or they didn't had access to it. Most of us feel that's a blessing for our patients. All of us here are salaried, but salary isn't determined by who we see, what we see, or by the volume of people we see. It's generated by our ability to look after people of different backgrounds well and reflects how we are reviewed.

We have specific awards in the physician community, including humanitarian awards, the most prized awards we give out. They identify people who have proven to go way beyond what is usual while looking out for everybody.

Dr. Bell: Did you receive cultural competency training prior to being on staff here at Cleveland Clinic?

Dr. Griffin: Not specifically. I've trained in a lot of different places and different parts of the country. To some degree, you have some cultural competency in the making but nothing formal, or even, informal. I learned from every place. Cedar Sinai Hospital in Beverly Hills had a big Jewish population. The Jewish population in Los Angeles is one of the largest in any city of the world and it was all centered near the hospital. I assimilated a lot of Jewish traditions and beliefs. This was good because I didn't have the same background as other people at the hospital. I was a minority because I wasn't Jewish. Nonetheless, I was very well looked after, and they were really nice to me. It gave me a great sense of what it's like if you are not the dominant culture in an institution or environment. That's not so bad for anybody. It's a good thing! We take a lot of things for granted when you are on the main screen or the dominant culture. When you are no longer in the dominant culture, you have to learn. Believe me, it's healthy. We have many different tribes, but we should easily relate to different strands. In the end, we're all human. People are not different. We share the same variety. People develop cultural identity but diversity of people within any identify is the same throughout.

Dr. Bell: Did you receive cultural competency coursework and/or training in medical school?

Dr. Griffin: I don't think so! I should have.

Dr. Bell: Which medical school did you go to?

Dr. Griffin: I went to a medical school in Ireland, but I doubt there was any cultural training.

Dr. Bell: So, we know how you feel about cultural competency...

Dr. Griffin: It's important for all of us to spend time outside of our comfort zones. That is a good thing about travel. When people travel to other countries, they are exposed to other cultures and gain life experiences not available in other ways.

Colleges and universities are now sending students for more and more years or semesters abroad. This is great because it allows young people to get outside their comfort zone in a new environment. When I spent a number of years training in a Boston city hospital, it was diverse and interesting. It was great exposure there to life that I've never seen before. There were a lot of impoverished people and a lot of potential violence. But it's great to see how many people are resilient to their environment and how good things come out of that resilience.

People like me who didn't have to worry about those things, found it good to see how blessed I've been. Medical school students who spend time in a city hospital in whatever city they are will benefit because they will see a lot.

Dr. Bell: Do you feel cultural competence is necessary in the medical practice to make a correct diagnosis and render a good treatment?

Dr. Griffin: It depends on your practice. People who are in an environment where they are very comfortable and comfortable with the people that they see fare well. If you are not in that type of practice, cultural competence is very important.

One of the key things about cultural competence is realizing what you don't know. If you are dealing with somebody from a completely different background from you, it's good to check with a colleague or a friend who understands that background very well. Is there something you are missing from their story? Often what seems like odd behavior to you may actually be very comprehensible to somebody who comes from the same or similar background.

Cultural competency isn't about being all things to all people because you can't achieve it. But always be humble enough to realize that sometimes you have to ask for help when you are dealing with people from other backgrounds. Am I missing the real issue here? Is there something I have forgotten? This goes beyond race or culture. Physicians often underestimate the financial burdens people have. If we prescribe something they can't pay for, they can't comply with treatment. That kind of competency and listening to the clues about those things is also very much needed. Some people will be very open and say "I have a big co-pay and I can't pay for this" and other people won't.

When we are being taught about competency, we need to be keenly aware of the prices of different medicines. This may be hard. You can see in the computer record what is paid for by the insurance company, but it doesn't tell you the co-pay or the true cost. Part of being competent too is if you say to someone who is really proud and maybe not that well off, can you afford to pay for this? That's not being competent either. It requires a lot of finesse to try to get to the bottom of the subject. You get better as you gain more experience. These are situations you don't think about enough when dealing with patients. Financial diversity is always relevant but we're not always aware of it. This could work both ways. You could be in an institution that prominently deals with people who are on Medicaid and assume they are covered just as easily as you could be in a hospital where you think everyone has private insurance and they are covered.

Dr. Bell: Do you view yourself as culturally competent?

Dr. Griffin: I work on it every day. Anybody who thinks they are culturally competent probably isn't.

Dr. Bell: What attitudes and characteristics do you possess that make you culturally competent?

Dr. Griffin: I'm interested in and enjoy people and their diversity. This doesn't make me culturally competent, but it makes me open to the idea that people are different and that's a good starting point. I naturally rejoice in diversity. It's fun and it's good. Ours would be a very boring place if we were all the same. We are all very similar. The character traits we see in our own tribe are replicated in another one. There's not much difference. It's a gift that we have diversity. The greatest thing about America is its diversity and ability to overcome. It's a society that respects what you can do rather than where you came from. Is it perfect? No, but there aren't a lot of societies that are. It's a can-do society so people can deliver. There are obstacles to people who have a lot to give but nonetheless, if people strive, there is something here for them. It's part of the United States of America. The majority of people want America to be diverse. Of course, there are those who disagree. But even from people you disagree with in politics, there's an overall sense that all men and women are created equal. Most people find this as the definition of the American experience--at least I hope so.

Dr. Bell: What are your thoughts about the value of cultural competence in the study, the research, and the practice of medicine in America?

Dr. Griffin: There's tremendous value. Embracing diversity should start in grade school. If this is something you are exposed to in medical school, then it's kind of late in the day. It's something we have to work on from the get-go. Some of it is about exposure. Part of me would say that medical training should involve having some experience in an underserved area. It's good for people to spend time in an environment where they are not the dominant culture. That makes you more competent to see things. I don't know how you would do that in training, but it definitely requires exposure. A lot of medical students are great and go and give back to the world. They go to different countries. They work as volunteers. We should keep that going.

Elisa P. Bell, M.D.

It's interesting when you have to reach outside of your own culture to somebody, and you have already been in a position where they are, or you are. It makes you more empathetic as to where people are. To some degree, the immigrant experience is that. When you come as an immigrant to this country, no matter who you are or how you arrived, there's a comfort level that you don't have. You haven't gone through grade school or done the pledge of allegiance. There are a lot of things you don't have. It's something for physicians and caregivers to see what it's like to be in the other person's shoes. If you have ever been sick and been in the hospital, it makes you more aware of loss of individuality and sometimes dignity and how institutionalized you become very quickly. This is an experience where most physicians see what it's like to be on the other side. I think the same way about the cultural thing. Maybe it's by roleplay or whatever but you have to see what it's like to be on the other side where you are no longer the dominant group, and it's good for you. It makes you listen more and give clues to people that say I'm here for you.

Dr. Bell: Well, thank you! Excellent! Culture is constantly changing.

Dr. Griffin: Culture is constantly changing. For the young folks, their culture is changing, too. Millennials view the world very differently from how Generation X and Baby Boomers view it. Instead of making it a value judgment, we need to understand the drivers that make these people act the way they do. Are they bad? Their priorities are different from what ours were and sometimes, that's actually quite good.

Dr. Bell: I really enjoyed this interview, thank you!

Elisa P. Bell, M.D.

Chapter Six

Discussing Cultural Competency

According the Terry L. Cross, Barbara J. Bazron, Karl W. Dennis, and Mareasa R. Isaacs, cultural competence is defined by the actions, belief systems, and operating principles of individuals and organizations. They describe a cultural competence spectrum that spans from cultural destructiveness to cultural proficiency. As health practitioners, a journey toward cultural proficiency must, in part, hinge on a desire to produce more effective results for the culturally diverse populations we serve. With this in mind, it is helpful to have a framework, such as the one provided by Terry L. Cross, et al., to help individual professionals and organizations examine where they are situated on the spectrum while they strive to become more culturally competent.

The outline below describes each of the six categories—in order from the least culturally competent to the most culturally competent—on the cultural competence spectrum.[29]

---

29   Terry L. Cross, et al., "Cultural Competence Continuum – Characteristics," *Coleman/Pellitory* (February 2013): http://www.eri-wi.org/download/conference/2013-conference/20_h_WhyDoesntEveryone_chart.pdf

Cultural Destructiveness:

My culture is the only culture that matters, and it is the most important.

An example of an attitude associated with cultural destructiveness includes, but is not limited to: My culture (group) is "the standard," "superior," "smarter," and "righteous" in contrast to other cultures (groups). So, it is acceptable—even justifiable—to harm people of other cultures (groups) because they are inferior and unworthy.

Cultural Incapacity:

I only look out and care for the people in my cultural group(s).

An example of an attitude associated with cultural incapacity includes, but is not limited to: An individual or group possesses an unconscious willingness to maintain the status quo by disproportionately giving resources to benefit their group. Thus, sending an indirect message to other groups that they are worthless and unwelcomed.

Cultural Blindness:

Regardless of culture, I believe all people are alike.

An example of an attitude associated with cultural blindness includes, but is not limited to: All people (groups) are the same. So, what is helpful for the dominate group applies to everyone. This thought assumes that the system is fair and achievement is based on merit.

Cultural Pre-competence:

I am aware of my culturally destructive attitudes, beliefs, and behavior and I want to learn how to strive for cultural competence.

An example of an attitude associated with cultural pre-competence includes, but is not limited to: this thinking tries to be inclusive, and it does not expect other people (groups) to assimilate to the dominate culture, while simultaneously being uninformed about how to respond to cultural differences when they are presented.

Cultural Competence:

I have an acceptance of difference that does not allow out casting, but promotes a sharing environment that is inclusive to all.

An attitude of cultural competence is observed by actions of commitment to social change and cultural equality, and it "Fosters mutual adaptation to differences to create environments that are useful for all."

Cultural Proficiency:

I greatly respect diverse cultures, identifying culture as the underpinning for effective, productive, and inclusive relationships with other people, groups, organizational structures, and systems.

An example of an attitude associated with cultural proficiency includes, but is not limited to thinking that realizes that people (groups) are separate and connected. With this realization, a meaningful mental shift occurs. So, the person (group) becomes more compassionate, constructive, and inclusive when interacting with people (groups) that are culturally different.

Observing Cross' cultural competency continuum characteristics should help a provider become more culturally sensitive: decreasing generalizations and one's willingness to adapt skills that allow a person to learn and understand about people from different cultures. This involves being aware of a set of similarities and differences that may exist in an individual who may be of a different cultural background.

Chapter Seven
Culture in Medicine

Culture has greatly influenced how societies practice medicine. From ancient times to present day, many factors such as religion, technology, politics, and economics influence medical practices. To understand these effects, I have provided a brief timeline of medical practice during antiquity BCE. The timeline allows one to understand and examine the evolution of cultural practices that were deemed necessary for the diagnosis of a disease, treatment, and resolution of illness.

Today, cultures throughout the world have different beliefs about illness and treatments. To provide culturally competent treatment to a group or culture of people, practitioners must try to understand the basics of a patient's cultural beliefs about illness and the healing process.

Throughout the world, some cultures have a different presentation of their illness that—by their standards—may require certain healing techniques. Practitioners should explore these differences through asking questions during diagnosis and treatment. Practitioners should not just focus on the disease, but also on the person. Some cultures today retain ancient medical practices, and still consider these practices necessary to treat or heal certain aliments or diseases. A medical practitioner's consideration and questioning about a patient's cultural beliefs, illness, and healing increases the probability of a more accurate diagnosis, and thus, a correct treatment.

In prehistoric times, herbal medicine was widely practiced. The herbalist was the healer. An herbalist is one who studies and uses plants in a medicinal manner. Appointed individuals, such as medicine men and shamans within certain ancient cultures, would administer herbal remedies to treat tribal members within the context of cultural practices, spiritual ceremonies, rituals, and magical powers. Herbalism is one of the oldest forms of medical practice. Some thought it was a gift from the gods. It was part of the culture that was passed down through generations. Earlier civilizations, like Egypt, Babylonia, China, and India left texts of their treatments that are still practiced today throughout the world.

The following is a brief timeline of medical practices during ancient BCE:

1. Prehistoric medicine—herbal medicine/it is said that the gods were the firsts herbalists/healers/physicians.

2. 3000 BC Egypt—official schools of the herbalists started here.

3. 2900 BC—Imhotep—he designed the step pyramid at Saqqara. The ancient Egyptian dean of medicine.[30] He practiced herbalism with faith healing and magic. He created the text known today as the Ewin Smith papyrus, a text on Egyptian treatments for diseases. It was found at Luxor in 1862. The Ebers papers, another ancient text, contained eight-hundred-and seventy-seven prescriptions and foul applications meant to turn away disease-causing demons. Around 2750 BC was

30   Carlos G. Musso, "Imhotep: The Dean among the Ancient Egyptian Physicians - an example of a Complete Physician," *Humane Medicine* 5, no.1 (2005): http://hekint.org/documents/AncientEgyptianPhysicians.pdf

the earliest known surgery in Egypt. Magic and religion were major parts of everyday life in Egypt.[31]

4. 2700 BC—China practiced herbalism. Shen-nung was considered the Father of Agriculture. He lived to the age one-hundred-and-twenty-three. Shen-nung used medicinal cannabis in 2737 BC, to treat gout and rheumatism. In 2600 BC, the Yellow Emperor rulers authored the Nei Ching Su Wen (book of internal medicine). This book is the basis of all Chinese medicine and is China's oldest medical book. [32]

5. 2500 CB—Babylonia's medical practices relied heavily on cultural practices—magic, astrology—with little scientific medicine. They learned herbal medicine from the Egyptians. They felt that the liver served as the life source of the body, both physically and spiritually. They attributed illnesses to angry gods.

6. 2000 BC—India-cultural medical practice used Veda—Vedas are filled with charms and practices for treatment of disease and to rid bodily demons. They used a wide variety of herbal treatments. Ayurveda is the science of life that was used in ancient times and is currently used in Indian cultures in the United States and throughout the world.

7. 1250 BC—Greek and Roman empires—the Greek schools of medicine owed much of their learning to the Egyptians. Hippocrates, Halophiles, and Galen studied at the temple of Amenhotep. They acknowledged the contribution of ancient Egyptian medicine to Greek medicine. In Greek religion and mythology Asclepius was a hero and the god

31   Ibid
32   Paul U. Unschuld, ed. Huang Di Nei Jing Su wen, *Nature, Knowledge, Imagery in an Ancient Chinese Medical Text:* http://www.acupunctureinsylva.com/uploads/2/7/9/6/27967113/huang_di_nei_jing_su_wen-paul_unschuld-2.pdf

of Greek medicine. His daughter Hygeia represented the practice of good hygiene, cleanses, asepsis, and good health. His daughter, Panacea, represented the goddess of healing during this period. The rod of Asclepius is a snake-entwined staff and remains the symbol of medicine today. A group of herb doctors were said to be a cult following of Aesculapius, which are thought to be the true founders of Greek medicine. They wrote the "magnificent oath of Aesculapius," which is now called the Hippocratic oath.

8. 536 BC—Jewish medicine—Jewish people were considered a separate race. They took very little herbal knowledge from the Egyptians. Their medicine was based on laws for prevention of illness. Their laws were transmitted by verbal tradition. Their herbal lore was compiled by King Solomon.

9. 450 BC—Hippocrates—the father of modern medicine. He was the first to practice modern medicine without reference to the gods. He was the first to separate superstition and magic from the practice of medicine. He stressed the need for the four humors of the body needing to be in balance, adding fresh air, a balanced diet, and exercise to help the body's natural healing process. Nature was dominant in Greek culture. They believed if one lives in concordance with nature, then good health will prevail; if an individual fails to do so, then disease will endure. The Greek culture was also influenced by their agricultural economy.

10. 350 BC—Aristotle—was a great philosopher and the first great biologist. His text the "de plantis" contained a list of over five hundred plants used in the healing process.

11. 50 AD—Pedanius Dioscorides—one of the greatest ancient herbalists wrote the text "de materia medica" of plants. It was

reprinted in 1933 and used as the chief source for herbalists for fifteen centuries.

12. 120 AD—Galen—he was named one of the greatest physicians in Ancient Greece. He was known to dissect animals and performed many operations. It was later proven by Andreas Vaesalis that some of Galen's work was incorrect. Because of Galen's monotheistic ideals and relationship with the Catholic Church, his work was thought to be authoritative and not questioned for many years. These medical practices prevailed in Europe for 1,800 years. A series of cultural changes occurred in the 16th century, dominance of Roman, Christianity, and Islamic conquests. This, in turn, led to the fall of Greek medical practices. During the Dark Ages, medicine went into decline, and medical superstition and ancient psychology was practiced. In 1000 AD, ancient medical knowledge began to return; there was the development of monastic medicine and medical schools. From the 1600s to the 21st century, modern/scientific medicine developed, the invention of x-rays, discovery of antibiotics, as well as the naming of disease-causing infections like tuberculosis, rabies, etc. Ultrasound and anesthetics were being used with the new emergence and great help of modern nursing. The twenty-first century ushered in the forefront of medicine and research became a part of the medical community.

History shows us that Western medicine has always been based on pure science, while alternative medicine uses methods such as acupuncture, herbalism, and aromatherapy, with its main focus being on the treatment of the mind, body, and spirit as one unit. This ancient approach is currently called a holistic doctor with a medical doctrine called naprapathy, a doctor of naprapathy with training in that discipline. Western medicine is practiced throughout the world. Within other countries as well as the United States, different cultures practice their ancient treatment modalities from the ancient times. Since the increase of multiculturalism in America, modern scientific medicine is being supplemented with alternative medical measures.

The ethnic makeup of America before the 19th century was mostly white, European immigrants. They maintained their sub-cultural identities, identifying themselves by race, ethnicity, language, religion, shared patterns, and beliefs. American institutions have educated and trained medical professionals by Western standards, leaving its imprints on how medical professionals respond to patients in all facets of care. During these earlier times, physicians practiced the credo "doctor knows best".

The dominant culture of white, Anglo-Saxon people maintained their socio-economic advantages. Still, after four hundred years of slavery on American soil, the African American population suffered the brunt of economic inequalities. As a result of these inequalities, illegal medical research was conducted on African Americans to benefit the dominant culture. Unethical studies were performed on African Americans before white people to the detriment of minorities. Examples include "the cloning of Henrietta Lacks' cells" and "the Tuskegee syphilis study." African Americans were used as test subjects without informed consent.

In the United States, the majority of doctors are of Anglo-European descent. History indicates this is due to systemic racism in American culture that supports and perpetuates cycles of poverty, racism, poor education, and trauma in urban communities. The majority of minorities reside in urban communities. Overall, the medical profession lacks diversity.

Doc, I have an earache.

2000 BC—Here, eat this root.

1000 BC—That root is a heathen, say this prayer.

1850 AD—Prayer is superstition, drink this potion.

1930 AD—That potion is snake oil, swallow this pill.

1970 AD—That pill is ineffective, take this antibiotic.

2000 AD—That antibiotic is artificial, here eat this root.

1. Carlos G. Musso, "Imhotep: The Dean among the Ancient Egyptian Physicians - an example of a Complete Physician," *Humane Medicine* 5, no.1 (2005): http://hekint. org/documents/AncientEgyptianPhysicians.pdf

2. ibid

3. Paul U. Unschuld, ed. Huang Di Nei Jing Su wen, *Nature, Knowledge, Imagery in an Ancient Chinese Medical Text:* http://www.acupunctureinsylva.com/ uploads/2/7/9/6/27967113/huang_di_nei_jing_su_wen-paul_unschuld-2.pdf

Chapter Eight

A Psychologist's Experience

Stanley Blom, PhD, Clinical Psychologist.

I came to understand cultural competency and diversity issues through the care, compassion, and sharing of information from several wonderful people in my life. These are people who listened, answered questions, and became my friends with no judgment on my ignorance, understanding that I grew to adulthood in a rather separate, homogenous community, affording me little exposure to people not culturally or ethnically like me.

My roots are in a small, rural, farming community where my family and friends were not only white, but ancestrally mostly from a small area of Northern Europe, the Netherlands. People of color were scarce in my community and were thought of as just other people. There was ignorance regarding people of color that was seen as acceptable. The neglect of others and our separateness was considered benign. So, there was no impetus to mingle with others or get to know the greater world. Not knowing people unlike ourselves, people from my school, church, and neighborhood thought that, of course, all people could and should get along. There was no appreciation that there were struggles "out there" raging because, in fact, people *did not* just get along. Further, the reasons for racial and cultural conflict had as much to do with overt racism as it had to do with communities—like mine— that practiced unawareness for those outside the community. This lack of awareness contributed critically and destructively to racism and suppression. Essentially, we lived in a white world and unthinkingly and, in most instances, unknowingly hoarded resources. As a result, people in my community thought all was well with the world, and, if it wasn't, then it must be because those for whom it wasn't well were doing something wrong. Only after living well outside of my childhood community and becoming intimately acquainted with people unlike my white, ordered community did I come to appreciate cultural and racial diversity, racial struggles, and white privilege.

The insular religious community where I developed in my childhood and teen years contained a curious and mutually exclusive pair of emphases: one was that our community and its members were better than most others and the second was that all people were equal in God's eyes. That these two appear from my later life vantage point to be mutually exclusive did not even come up for discussion or recognition in those early years. There was such a pervasive, assumed attitude toward people from outside the community that no thought was given to introspection. I've come to understand my community to be operating from an essentialist perspective, i.e., believing that racial differences and characteristics attributed to races are inherent and fixed. Essentialism blames the "other," i.e., blames "not my race" and views racial differences and racism to be unavoidable. What many more people now understand by now is that race is a social construct, i.e., race and attendant stereotypes are not based on genetic makeup. They are instead the result of societal ideologies and people who believe in them to attribute certain characteristics to particular races. In fact, constructivism understands racism as arising out of societal

Elisa P. Bell, M.D.

ideologies and societal norms rather than on genetics. DNA does not serve as a reason to distinguish or discriminate between races in any way relevant to human activity.

There are many people, especially those of color, to whom I owe tremendous gratitude and deep debts for loving me and sharing of themselves, their histories, struggles, and pains without taking offense at my lack of understanding and countless questions. While my background left me entering adult life with little awareness of my ignorance, a religious emphasis in my formative years on viewing all humans as alike and equally valuable with no pride simply arising from genetics was beneficial because it propelled me toward a deeper understanding of others. Thus, I was fortunate—through no choice of my own—to be open to hearing and seeing what others were like without judgment.

Two of the four most helpful people for me, as I became more aware and informed regarding people of color, were a pair of educators with whom I worked shortly after earning my bachelor's degree. I served for several years in an urban school for students with emotional struggles and learning disabilities. Many of those students and the two fellow educators were African American. This was my first opportunity to work closely with persons from a very different background. These persons grew up in an urban community. They were also nonjudgmental, unstinting in their support, and accepting. So, I could not help but return the generosity. Even though I arrived with preconceived notions—some unpleasant and some benign, but nonetheless offensive—I was soon relaxed, accepted, and able to open myself to knowledge and relationships. I was able to see persons, and not figures of my own presuppositions. I learned about what it was like to grow to maturity and live in a predominantly African American culture. I found that my biases were much more prevalent from me toward the people with whom I worked than theirs were toward me. This may be the result of me having lived a life, until then, of little interaction with African American people. Thus, I had little opportunity or urge to learn about others. On the other hand, African Americans grow up as the minority culture, having to learn early how to make sense out of the non-African American, white culture, i.e., my coworkers knew much more about whites than I did about blacks. I learned about the importance of family authority figures, holding children and grand-children accountable with seemingly strict and harsh guidance and punishments arising from with deep affection and fear of children running afoul of the powers that were in the dominant, white cul-ture. I began to understand and appreciate a culture wherein family and responsibility extended to not only parent-child relationships but included grandparents, aunts, uncles, cousins, neighbors, and church members. I had grown up in a community where nuclear family parents and children often insulated themselves from direct outside commentary and commands: to see extended family and non-relatives wield authority as I only had seen in nuclear families was illuminating. As I learned about African American culture, I developed a recognition of my white privilege, something I did not know existed, but came to realize had been there all along.

Another key person in my life was a mentor, supervisor, profes-sor, and friend during my graduate school time in Detroit. He also was one to answer all my questions, encourage me with information and answers to questions I did not even know I had. He has since passed away, but at the time I knew him, he was the most widely read, brilliant, strong, and curious person I had ever met. He was African American. He entertained all my fumbling questions, again with equanimity and nonjudgment. This mentor explained the history of African American culture in America, and especially in Detroit. There are subtle and not so subtle nuances I came to appreciate among African Americans in Detroit and across the country. I came to understand that there were minute, but important differences between African American residents who lived in different neighborhoods, even in different blocks of the city. Also, he explained the deep and rich history of Africans not only in America but in the ancestral continent. In talking with this mentor, I was stimulated to learn more about African history. He patiently explained how the culture of Africa was largely ignored in Western civilization and in Western treatises on history when, in fact, the African continent, especially West Africa, was the epitome of highly advanced civilizations during the European Dark Ages. That is, when European civilization collapsed and regressed to rather primitive status, African empires, politics, governance, science, art, literature, math, astronomy, architecture, wealth, power, and gender equality were so highly advanced that Europe did not begin to catch up until the European Renaissance. So dark was Europe and so enlightened was Africa that some European elite sent their youth to African universities to gain genuine education. This information and the facts to support it were readily available, but overlooked by most white people, including myself. When I began to explore this history it profoundly changed how I viewed Africans, African Americans, and any person outside my culture of origin. I realized that my culture was not exceptional, or maybe it is but others are, also. It gave me an appreciation for the vitality, equality, and value of all people, especially African Americans. To be in the acquaintance of this mentor, be accepted, be educated, and be appreciated for myself was powerful and prompted me to do all that and more for others. I cannot thank him enough--he helped me gain awareness and appreciate the worth and uniqueness of all of us.

Finally, perhaps the most influential person in my life as I traveled this path is a good friend from whom I have learned a tremendous amount about African American culture and the nuances and sensibilities of the lives of blacks in America. The person to whom I refer is Dr. Elisa P. Bell. She has shared her personal history, including the wonderful, loving family background, as well as the struggles and pains while succeeding against the wishes and strategies of too many in the dominant, white culture. I came to more deeply understand and appreciate African American culture and white culture, and how these two were variously able to work well together, but many times were far apart and in intense conflict. At one point, I suggested that had I faced what Elisa had to face, I would likely have been extremely angry and in violent revolt. Eventually, I also came to understand how that response has its place, but some choose other paths for understandable reasons. Understanding another's culture has left me deeply appreciative, humbled, advocatory, and grateful to have the good fortune to meet and become friends with these and other people.

Chapter Nine
Final Words

This book represents a new beginning on a journey of self-discovery, starting the process of each clinician's examination of self. Each clinician can explore their ancestral past, their current culture, as well as the culture of others. In so doing, the outcome should yield a deeper understanding of one's cultural beliefs and biases.

This book gives insight into how we look at ourselves as well as other diverse groups and their cultures. As health professionals, we must be curious to learn about different cultures, beliefs, attitudes, rituals, and languages--to signal the start of our journey to cultural competency.

We are part of a multicultural society with different approaches to embrace and treat illness. When we understand and learn about people from different cultures, we equip ourselves to understand their illness and have a better chance to render more accurate diagnoses and treatments. The book shows an abbreviated historic timeline about how culture influences treatment.

My hope is that—by discussing national standards and offering personal case histories from skilled clinicians—readers and clinicians will own a catalyst to become more culturally competent. Culture remains dynamic and evolves at lightning speed. Consequently, becoming culturally competent is a lifelong process for continuous learning.

By the year 2050, two-thirds of Americans will be minorities and ninety percent will live in urban settings. As clinicians, we have an obligation to educate ourselves about changing populations, including, but not limited to LGBT, elderly, and minority.

In preparing this book, I've shared my early processes to understand culture throughout my childhood and adolescent years. I offered my community, and I identified myself through my race and culture. I discussed various experiences and people I encountered while traveling around the globe. My experiences changed my perspective on self and the world around me.

After interviewing Dr. Griffin, I now have a deeper understanding of how he processes the world around him and the people he encounters. I also have a better understanding of culture as it pertains to diagnosis and treatment. When Dr. Griffin did not understand a barrier within a culture, he deferred to his peers, asking questions to better understand a patient while rendering a correct diagnosis and treatment. I ask you to examine his story again, as I find it to be a great example of cultural competency.

After examining the NCCC Website, I visited Tawara Goode to get a better grasp of cultural competency from someone who is an expert in the field. She approaches cultural competency holistically, including language as part of proficiency in cultural competency.

She gives the complete definition of cultural competency, using T. Cross' six steps to cultural competency. She expands the definition to systems and organizations to look within communities to engage diverse groups. She shows us a continuum to develop more cultural competency.

I continue to engage in the practice of becoming culturally competent. I examine self and ask questions with humility, empathy, and respect to gain a richer understanding of the patients I serve/treat. I learn from each encounter what best serves my patients. I have to be patient and listen. I try my best to understand their ways/beliefs and incorporate their methods as best I can. I must allow them to be part of the decision-making team.

Allow me to share another personal story. For many years, I have suffered from chronic sinus infections. I 've had many infections in the past, and was treated with standard antibiotic medications. In 2000, I had sinus surgery, and it relieved my chronic infections for many years, until 2015. Since then I had many rounds of antibiotics with intermittent relief, and recently, I had a severe sinus infection. I was treated with a ten-day regimen of a strong antibiotic, and it resolved in ten days. On the sixteenth day, my infection returned with bronchitis. A friend suggested I see a fourth-generation Chinese herbalist.

The herbalist gave me tea to drink for twelve days. I was open to trying this healing process. Another friend, who is a physician, suggested an acupuncturist (Naprapathy) for treatment. Because of my experience writing this book, I tried these other healing processes – with success. My visits to China, South Korea, and Thailand to explore their healing practices provided research for the book and opened my mind to new healing methods.

Today, medical practices include natural/functional/holistic medicine. Since the 1970s, society has progressed to combine natural healing with traditional medicine. This care is more popular and accepted due to cultural influence, economics, diversity, and acceptance.

I challenge you, readers/clinicians, to enhance your practice by daring to understand who you are--your self-identity, biases, cultural beliefs, and affinity for diverse groups—to achieve cultural competency. The first step: acknowledge the need to self-identify and discover unknowns; learn, understand, embrace, accept differences, and serve diverse groups. For some people, this book can serve as the beginning for becoming more culturally competent. Good luck on your journey.

Elisa P. Bell, M.D.

About the Author

Elisa P. Bell, MD, is a distinguished alumna of Southern Illinois University School of Medicine. Soon after graduating from medical school, she completed an internship in Pediatrics at Loyola Medical Center, an adult residency in psychiatry at Illinois State Psychiatric Institute, as well as a fellowship in child psychiatry at University of Michigan Hospital in Ann Arbor, Michigan. In 2017, she practiced Telemedicine Psychiatry, providing psychiatric care to juveniles at the Third District Circuit Court in Detroit, Michigan. In South Bend, Indiana, and Springfield, Illinois she trained a host of professionals on cultural competency.

Currently, she is a full-time staff Adult Psychiatrist at the Illinois Department of Corrections, Northern Reception Center. She is also an associate professor of Child/Adolescent Psychiatry at Rush University, where she gives cultural competency lectures to audiences of residents, medical students, and child psychiatry fellows.

Dr. Bell is hailed by peers as a gifted psychiatrist, and she is known as a "community psychiatrist" due to her interest in and dedication to the Chicago community. Her patient care and community service include educating communities about mental illness. She established a panel discussion on the negative effects of lead poisoning in children, telecast in the Chicago area. In addition, she served as a spokesperson for the Human Animal Violence Connection (HAVC), having featured on CBS News, CLTV News, FOX News in the Morning with Tamara Hall, and Channel 9 News, a local Chicagoland area channel. She has been featured locally in newspapers and served as a guest on several local call-in radio shows, answering questions about the mental health of children and adolescents. During the Clinton Administration, she participated as a panelist on a national teleconference with President Bill Clinton and First Lady Hillary Clinton, discussing the state of youth.

On November 2, 2008, Dr. Bell was the featured guest speaker at the NAACP/Freedom Fund Banquet, where she spoke on the theme "Power, Justice, Freedom and Voting."

In 2005, Dr. Bell organized and developed a crisis intervention team at Trinity United Church of Christ to help students who were victims of Hurricane Katrina. Moreover, she was instrumental in developing a pilot study of African-American females with asthma for the state of Illinois. While chairperson of Mental Health for the Urban Health Initiative at the University of Chicago, she wrote the mental health section of a grant for the Woodlawn Zone Project.

In 2001, Dr. Bell was a guest speaker at the Annual Research Conference at the University of Chicago. Her topic was "Mental Health Treatment Issues for African-American Males." Spearheading the Autism Parent Advocacy Group (PANS-G) in Northwest Indiana, Dr. Bell worked with parents, helping them understand the prevalence and diagnosis of autism in the United States. She also served seven years on the board for the Chicagoland Autism Connection.

Dr. Bell's awards are numerous, and include, but are not limited to, the following: Distinguished Alumna for Iowa Wesleyan University, Distinguished Alumna for Southern Illinois University School of Medicine, Community Service Award for Alpha Kappa Alpha Sorority:

Southside Service Awards, and induction into the Illinois State Martial Arts Hall of Fame Community Service.